I0759620

IT'S TIME TO BAKE

pastries

BRIAN HART HOFFMAN

83 press®

IT'S TIME TO BAKE
pastries
an introduction
to pâtisserie

83 Press
2323 2nd Avenue North
Birmingham, Alabama 35203
83press.com

ISBN: 979-8-9899185-5-3
Printed in China

contents

A Passion for Pastry

It was during my first career as a flight attendant that I fell in love with all things pastry while I wandered through the arrondissements of Paris. The sight of perfectly aligned éclairs and piles of pearl sugar-clad chouquettes was captivating. Being immersed in a culture that embraces and revolves around the timeless art of making pastry inspired me to dedicate my second career to sugar and butter and to sharing the joy that comes from baking something delicious for those I love.

This collection will transport you into the magical world of pastry. It's filled with a treasure trove of recipes—each with its own story to tell—from my culinary travels, where I discovered delectable pastries to re-create in my kitchen. My craving to learn and educate passionate bakers echoes throughout these pages as I dive deep into the intricate details and in-depth techniques of the various types of pastry, explaining how different ingredients interact with one another and how specific techniques can transform fat and flour into a unique experience.

Each chapter introduces a different style of foundational French pastry, each with endless possibilities. Confidently conquer pâte feuilletée, and you'll be whipping up golden morning buns, tarte tatins, kouign amann, and more. Learn how to make pâte viennoise, and you'll be able to create gorgeous, flaky croissants, delightful Danish, and perfectly balanced brioche! By mastering different types of pastry, you will soon be on your way to creating exquisite pâtisserie delights at home.

I believe that pastries should be a symphony of incredible taste, be easy to achieve, and allow your creativity to shine through. This cookbook is your guide to enhancing your pastry-making confidence and provides the knowledge you need to succeed, whether you're a seasoned professional or a passionate home baker who delights in creating something delicious from scratch.

It's time to bake!

Brian

What Is Pastry?

The term "pastry" represents a divine assortment of beautifully crafted baked goods, each a unique expression of flavor and texture. These delectable delights are created from flour and fat along with sugar, milk, water, eggs, and leavening agents, resulting in a magical culinary transformation. The charm of pastry lies in its exquisite and refined appearance, ranging from flaky, buttery croissants to decadent cream-filled éclairs. Within these pages, you can delve into the fundamental types of pastry dough—each possessing distinctive characteristics and versatile applications—that serve as the foundation for an array of irresistible pastries.

Pâte Feuilletée (PUFF PASTRY)

Classic puff pastry is comprised of a flour-and-water dough and butter that is repeatedly folded and rolled out, creating distinct and delicate layers. During baking, these layers unfurl to reveal air pockets throughout the pastry, producing numerous light, flaky layers. This unique combination achieves a balance of tenderness and crispiness. Rough puff, an inventive variation of classic puff pastry, involves incorporating large butter pieces into a dough, offering a less precise but equally captivating method. Puff pastry is an elegant and versatile choice for an array of indulgent bakes, from the appeal of *palmiers* to the splendor of *chaussons aux pommes* (apple turnovers).

Pâte Friable (CRUMBLY DOUGH)

These unleavened doughs form the base for pies, tarts, and quiches. *Pâte brisée* (broken pastry) is the simplest style of crumbly dough, consisting solely of flour, water, salt, and butter. *Pâte sucrée* (sweet pastry) provides subtle sweetness and richness through the addition of sugar and eggs, resulting in a delicate, crisp texture. *Pâte sablée* (sandy pastry) is the most indulgent, and its buttery richness often requires gently pressing it into a pie or tart pan rather than rolling it out.

Pâte Viennoise

Originating in Vienna, Austria, this yeast-leavened dough made its mark in France when August Zang, an Austrian military official, opened Boulangerie Viennoise in Paris in 1839, ushering in a new era of innovation in French pastry culture. These pastries are typically made with flour and yeast, which causes the dough to rise rapidly, producing the flawless flakiness that defines its signature allure. These breakfast pastries, reminiscent of bread but sweeter and more indulgent, include the intricate golden layers of croissants, kringles, and *pain suisse*.

Pâte à Choux (CHOUX PASTRY)

Pâte à choux is a wonderfully versatile dough created from water, butter, flour, eggs, and a little sugar. “Choux,” pronounced like “shoo,” comes from the French word for cabbage due to choux puffs’ resemblance to miniature cabbage heads after baking. Distinguished by its unique preparation method, this dough is cooked twice: once on the stovetop and again during baking or frying. The dough’s high moisture content causes it to delightfully puff up as it bakes, resulting in a light and airy interior with a crisp exterior, perfect for filling with luscious cream for *choux au craquelin* or dredging in cinnamon sugar for decadent churros.

Pâte Battue (BEATEN DOUGH) and Pâte Tournée (TURNED DOUGH)

These doughs are a family of leavened batters, often crafted by incorporating air into the mixture through rigorous beating or whipping, producing a light and ethereal texture. *Pâte génoise* is a variety of *pâte battue* used for iconic shell-shaped madeleines and elaborate confections like the illustrious opera cake. The term “génoise” comes from the French word for Genoa, Italy, where this style of cake batter likely originated, and it has become a key component of many French pastries.

PRONUNCIATION GUIDE

Battue (BA-too)

Boulangerie (boo-lahn-zhuh-ree)

Brisée (bree-zay)

Chaussons aux pommes (SHOW-sahn oh PUM)

Choux (shoo)

Craquelin (kra-kuh-lan)

Croquembouche (kroh-kum-boosh)

Feuilletée (fuh-yuh-tay)

Financiers (fee-nahn-syay)

Friable (FREE-abl)

Galette des rois (GAL-et deh rWAH)

Gâteau (GA-toh)

Boulangerie, Pâtisserie, or Viennoiserie?

Boulangerie: A boulangerie is the heart and soul of a French bakery, where the comforting aroma of freshly baked bread lures you in. While pâtisserie and viennoiserie may also grace the shelves, bread takes the spotlight, from the iconic baguette to traditional French loaves.

Pâtisserie: Entering a pâtisserie is like stepping into a magical realm dedicated to the art of confectionery. Here, a dazzling array of delights awaits, from the intricate layers of mille-feuilles to the dainty elegance of petit fours and the vibrant hues of macarons.

Viennoiserie: Inspired by the traditions of Vienna, Austria, viennoiseries embody the harmony between pastry and bread. Viennoiseries beckon with irresistibly captivating breakfast pastries, from buttery croissants and flaky Danish to plush brioche.

Génoise (ZHAYN-wahz)

Gougères (goo-zhair)

Kouign amann (kween ah-mahn)

Langues de chat (LAHNG duh sha)

Mille-feuille (meal-foy)

Pain suisse (pan swees)

Palmiers (pal-mee-yay)

Paris-Brest (pah-ree brest)

Pâte (pat)

Pâtisserie (pa-tis-uh-ree)

Sablée (sah-blay)

Sucrée (soo-kray)

Tarte Tatin (tart ta-tan)

Tournée (toor-nay)

Viennoise (vyehn-wahz)

Viennoiserie (vyehn-wahz-uh-ree)

Essential Pastry Ingredients and Equipment

Ingredients

Through my culinary journey, I've learned the valuable lesson of cherishing my ingredients. Whether it's the exquisite flavor of a perfectly ripe satsuma or the aromatic richness of Saigon cinnamon, quality ingredients are the foundation of exceptional pastries. This book encourages you to honor and embrace the finest ingredients, ensuring your pastry is a true culinary masterpiece.

EUROPEAN-STYLE BUTTER

ALL-PURPOSE FLOUR, BREAD FLOUR, CAKE FLOUR

GRANULATED SUGAR, BROWN SUGAR, CONFECTIONERS' SUGAR

KOSHER SALT

EGGS

WHOLE MILK

HEAVY WHIPPING CREAM

YEAST

Equipment

One of my guiding principles in the kitchen is to use the right tools for the job. A well-designed tool is not just a utensil; it's a source of inspiration that can transform your baking experience. These fundamental tools will not only enhance your baking but also empower you in the kitchen.

DIGITAL SCALE

GLASS MIXING BOWLS

MEASURING SPOONS

INSTANT-READ THERMOMETER

PARCHMENT PAPER

BAKING SHEETS

CAKE PANS

WIRE RACKS

BENCH SCRAPER

FINE-MESH SIEVE

PASTRY BLENDER

PASTRY BRUSH

PASTRY CUTTER/WHEEL

OFFSET SPATULA

SILICONE SPATULA

ROLLING PIN

RULER

WHISK

PASTRY BAGS

PIPING TIPS

KITCHEN SHEARS

CHEF'S KNIFE

PARING KNIFE

SERRATED KNIFE

SAUCEPAN

pâte feuilletée

puff pastry dough

TARTE TATIN, MILLE-FEUILLES, PALMIERS

The repeated folding and rolling of puff pastry dough creates distinct flaky layers that bake up soft yet crisp. Whether you choose classic puff pastry or its simplified variation, rough puff pastry, each will more than reward your time and effort.

Classic Puff Pastry Dough

Light and crisp, buttery and indulgent, this pastry can be the base of a seemingly infinite number of creations.

4 cups (508 grams) bread flour
1½ teaspoons (4.5 grams) kosher salt
5 tablespoons (70 grams) cold unsalted butter, cubed
1¼ cups (300 grams) ice water
1 tablespoon (15 grams) fresh lemon juice
1½ cups (340 grams) unsalted butter, softened
⅓ cup (42 grams) all-purpose flour, plus more for dusting

1. In the bowl of a stand mixer, whisk together bread flour and salt by hand. Add cold butter; using the paddle attachment, beat at low speed until butter has worked into flour and mixture resembles cornmeal.
2. In a liquid-measuring cup, combine 1¼ cups (300 grams) ice water and lemon juice. With mixer on low speed, slowly add lemon water to flour mixture, beating just until combined. Switch to the dough hook attachment, and beat at medium-low speed until dough is smooth and elastic, 4 to 5 minutes.
3. Lightly dust work surface with all-purpose flour; turn out dough onto prepared surface, and shape into a 1-inch-thick square. Wrap in plastic wrap, and refrigerate until ready to use or for at least 30 minutes.
4. Clean bowl of stand mixer and paddle. Using the paddle attachment, beat softened butter and all-purpose flour at low speed until smooth and well combined, 2 to 3 minutes.
5. Draw a 9-inch square on a piece of parchment paper; turn parchment over. (Draw square dark enough to be seen through other side of parchment.) Spread butter mixture in an even layer on prepared parchment within edges of square. Fold paper over butter mixture, or top with another piece of parchment. Refrigerate until firm, at least 30 minutes.
6. Roll dough into a 12-inch square. Place cold butter square diagonally in center of dough so that four corners of dough are visible. Fold corners of dough over butter to meet in center, pinching seams to seal.
7. Lightly dust dough and a rolling pin with all-purpose flour. Using rolling pin, lightly tap dough into a rectangle. Roll dough into a 20x10-inch rectangle. Brush off excess flour. Fold dough in thirds like a letter. (This is called a trifold.) Rotate dough 90 degrees so one long side is now closest to you.
8. Roll dough into a 20x10-inch rectangle, with one long side closest to you. Fold dough in half so short sides meet; gently press dough at fold to mark center. Unfold dough. Fold short sides of dough to meet in center of dough; fold one half of dough onto other half of dough as if you are closing a book. (This is called a book-fold.) Wrap dough in plastic wrap, and refrigerate for 30 minutes.
9. Repeat rolling and folding procedure for 2 more book-folds, refrigerating dough for at least 30 minutes after each fold. (You should complete a total of 1 trifold and 3 book-folds.) Wrap dough in plastic wrap, and refrigerate for at least 1 hour or up to 2 days.

pro tip

Puff pastry dough can also be frozen, tightly wrapped, for up to 2 months. Let it thaw overnight in the refrigerator before using.

Unfolding Puff Pastry

Puff pastry is made using a process called lamination, which means a block of butter, called the *beurrage*, is tightly wrapped and sealed in a block of dough, called the *détrempe*. When combined, the bundle is called the *pâton*. The pastry gets its height and lightness through a series of rolls and folds. The first fold creates luscious, alternating layers of dough and butter. The remaining folds create the pastry's numerous intricate layers. As the pastry bakes, the butter melts and the moisture inside evaporates, pushing the flaky dough upward. I show every step of "the puff" so you can master this pastry like a pro.

Making the Dough

In the bowl of a stand mixer, whisk together flour and salt. Add cold cubed butter; using the paddle attachment, beat at low speed until butter has worked into flour and mixture resembles cornmeal. In a liquid-measuring cup, combine 1¼ cups (300 grams) ice water and lemon juice. With mixer on low speed, slowly add lemon water to flour mixture, beating just until combined. Switch to the dough hook attachment, and beat at medium-low speed until dough is smooth and elastic, 4 to 5 minutes.

TIP: The acidity from the lemon juice helps create a more tender crust as the acid reacts with the flour and the fat from the butter to create a lighter, flaky texture.

Turn out dough out onto a lightly floured surface, and pat into a 1-inch-thick square. Wrap in plastic wrap, and refrigerate until ready to use or for at least 30 minutes.

TIP: Shaping the dough into a uniform square will make it easier to roll out later before adding the butter block.

Forming the Butter Block

Clean bowl of stand mixer and paddle. Using the paddle attachment, beat softened butter and all-purpose flour at low speed until smooth and well combined, 2 to 3 minutes.

TIP: The small amount of flour in the butter block helps the butter stay pliable and keeps it from breaking up in the dough.

Draw a 9-inch square on a piece of parchment paper; turn parchment over. (Draw square dark enough to be seen through other side of parchment.) Spread butter mixture in an even layer on prepared parchment within edges of square. Fold paper over butter, or top with another piece of parchment. Refrigerate until firm, at least 30 minutes.

TIP: Before lamination, your butter and dough should be close to the same pliability for easy lamination. Move butter or dough to room temperature or to the freezer as needed to achieve this.

Roll dough into a 12-inch square. Place cold butter square diagonally in center of dough so four corners of dough are visible. Fold corners of dough over butter to meet in center, pinching seams to seal.

TIP: This step is referred to as "the lock-in," and it ensures the butter is properly sealed inside the dough.

Creating the Layers

Lightly flour dough and rolling pin. Using rolling pin, lightly tap dough into a rectangular shape. Roll dough into a 20x10-inch rectangle. Brush off excess flour. Fold dough in thirds like a letter. (This is called a trifold.) Rotate dough 90 degrees so one long side is now closest to you.

TIP: If you are struggling to get your dough to roll out for the folds, just cover and refrigerate for an additional 20 to 30 minutes and try again. Lamination is hard work, and the dough (and you!) will need some rest.

Roll dough into a 20x10-inch rectangle, with one long side closest to you. Fold dough in half so short sides meet; lightly press dough at fold to mark center. Unfold dough. Fold short sides of dough to meet in center. Fold one half of dough onto other half of dough as if you are closing a book. (This is called a book-fold.) Wrap dough in plastic wrap, and refrigerate for 30 minutes.

TIP: Always work with fridge-cold dough. During shaping, if the dough gets too warm, the butter will start to melt into the dough, and you will lose your lamination. If it's taking too long to shape or if you have hot hands, take a break and refrigerate the dough until it's firm again.

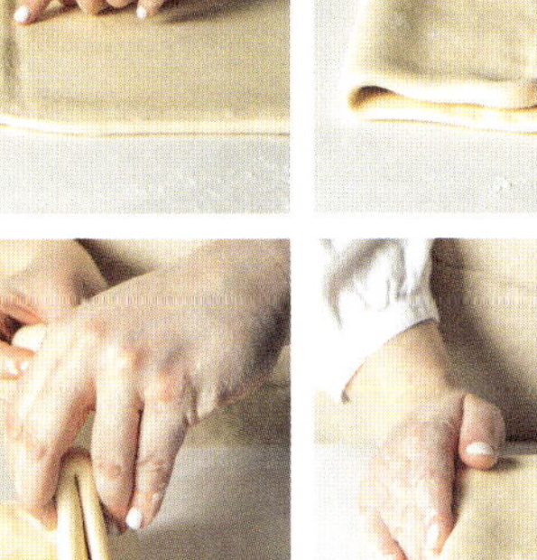

Repeat rolling, folding, and rotating procedure for 2 more book-folds, refrigerating dough for at least 30 minutes after each fold. (You should complete a total of 1 trifold and 3 book-folds.) Wrap dough in plastic wrap, and refrigerate for at least 1 hour or up to 2 days.

TIP: Keeping the dough cold will help maintain the ideal temperature for folding.

Apple Tarte Tatin

Makes 1 (12-inch) tart

The tarte Tatin was born in the late 19th century at the Hotel Tatin in Lamotte-Beuvron, a small village in the heart of the Loire Valley in France. Created to salvage overcooked (and caramelized) apples, it has grown to become one of the most celebrated and recognizable of all French desserts. Making a good apple tarte Tatin is all about technique since the ingredients are simple. Choosing an apple that holds its shape well is also important.

All-purpose flour, for dusting
Classic Puff Pastry Dough (recipe on page 18)
7 to 8 medium Honeycrisp or other sweet apples (1,200 to 1,300 grams), peeled, halved, cored, and cut into ¾-inch-thick slices
3 tablespoons (45 grams) fresh lemon juice
¾ cup (150 grams) granulated sugar
¼ cup (57 grams) cold unsalted butter, cubed
¾ teaspoon (4.5 grams) vanilla bean paste or (3 grams) vanilla extract
Crème fraîche, to serve

1. Preheat oven to 400°F (200°C).
2. On a lightly floured sheet of parchment paper, roll Classic Puff Pastry Dough into a 12-inch circle (about ⅛ inch thick); refrigerate.
3. In a large bowl, toss together apples and lemon juice.
4. In a 12-inch ovenproof skillet, sprinkle sugar in an even layer. Cook over medium heat, without stirring, until sugar begins to melt, 2 to 4 minutes. Reduce heat to medium-low, and whisk sugar just to slightly break up any lumps. Cook, without stirring, until sugar is light amber in color, about 5 minutes. Remove from heat; add cold butter, and swirl skillet to melt.
5. Return skillet to heat; add apples and vanilla bean paste or extract. Cook over medium heat, gently stirring and turning, until apples soften and start to turn translucent at edges, about 10 minutes. Remove from heat; let cool slightly.
6. Transfer apples to a heatproof bowl. Using tongs and starting at sides of skillet, arrange apples in concentric circles to fully cover, overlapping as needed. Pour any liquid from bowl onto apples in skillet. Place pastry on apples, tucking in edges all around apples. Cut 3 slits in pastry to let steam escape. Place skillet on a baking sheet.
7. Bake until pastry is golden brown and juices are bubbling around edges, 30 to 35 minutes, rotating skillet halfway through baking. Let cool in skillet on a wire rack for 15 to 20 minutes.
8. Carefully invert tart onto a serving plate. Serve immediately with crème fraîche.

Orange Custard Bars

Makes 10 to 12 servings

Sophisticated meets doable in this dessert of creamy custard sandwiched between flaky layers of homemade puff pastry. Dress it up with whipped cream and fresh fruit.

Classic Puff Pastry Dough (recipe on page 18)
All-purpose flour, for dusting
3½ cups (840 grams) plus 4 tablespoons (60 grams) heavy whipping cream, divided
1½ cups (300 grams) plus 2 tablespoons (24 grams) granulated sugar, divided
¾ cup (96 grams) cornstarch
3½ cups (840 grams) whole milk
6 large egg yolks (112 grams)
1 tablespoon (2 grams) orange zest
¼ cup (57 grams) unsalted butter
3 tablespoons (45 grams) orange liqueur
¼ teaspoon kosher salt
Garnish: confectioners' sugar

1. Preheat oven to 400°F (200°C).
2. Divide Classic Puff Pastry Dough in half. On a lightly floured piece of parchment paper, roll half of dough into a 16x12-inch rectangle. (Keep remaining dough refrigerated.) Transfer dough on parchment to an 18x13-inch rimmed baking sheet.
3. Brush 2 tablespoons (30 grams) cream onto dough on pan; sprinkle 1 tablespoon (12 grams) granulated sugar onto cream. Place a piece of parchment paper on dough; top with another 18x13-inch baking sheet.
4. Bake until golden brown, 20 to 22 minutes, pressing down on center of top pan halfway through baking to release air from pastry. Press down on pan again, and remove top pan and parchment paper; let cool completely on pan.
5. Repeat procedure with remaining dough, 2 tablespoons (30 grams) cream, and 1 tablespoon (12 grams) granulated sugar.
6. In a large saucepan, whisk together cornstarch and remaining 1½ cups (300 grams) granulated sugar. Gradually whisk in milk and remaining 3½ cups (840 grams) cream until smooth. Heat over medium heat, whisking frequently, just until bubbles form around sides of pan. (Do not boil.)
7. In a medium bowl, whisk together egg yolks and orange zest. Gradually add 2 cups hot milk mixture to egg yolk mixture, whisking constantly. Whisk egg yolk mixture into remaining hot milk mixture in pan. Cook over medium heat, whisking constantly, until thickened and bubbly.
8. Remove from heat; whisk in butter, liqueur, and salt until butter is melted and mixture is well combined. Let stand at room temperature for 10 minutes. Transfer to a bowl, and cover with plastic wrap, pressing wrap directly onto surface of custard to prevent a skin from forming.
9. Line a 13x9-inch baking pan with parchment paper, letting excess extend over sides of pan. Using a pastry cutter or pastry wheel, trim sides of pastry sheets to make 13x9-inch rectangles. Place one pastry sheet in prepared pan. Gently pour warm custard on pastry. Top with remaining pastry sheet, gently pressing down. Refrigerate until custard is cold, thick, and set, at least 4 hours, or up to overnight.
10. Using excess parchment as handles, gently remove from pan. Using a serrated knife, gently cut into squares. Garnish with confectioners' sugar, if desired. Refrigerate in an airtight container for up to 2 days. Best served same day as made.

Mille-Feuilles

Makes 12 pastries

Meaning "a thousand sheets" in French, the mille-feuille is known for its seemingly countless layers of puff pastry. With a buttery vanilla pastry cream, my Mille-Feuilles are simple yet decadent. I bake the dough layered between two rimmed baking sheets stacked on top of each other so the pastry is flat and level to build up its famous layers.

All-purpose flour, for dusting
Classic Puff Pastry Dough (recipe on page 18)
Confectioners' sugar, for dusting
Vanilla Bean Crème Mousseline (recipe follows)
Fresh berries, to serve

1. Preheat oven to 400°F (200°C). Line 2 rimmed baking sheets with parchment paper.
2. On a lightly floured surface, roll Classic Puff Pastry Dough into a 24½x12½-inch rectangle (about ⅛ inch thick). Using a pastry wheel, trim ¼ inch off all sides of rectangle. Cut dough into 36 (4x2-inch) rectangles. Place rectangles at least ½ inch apart on prepared pans. Place another sheet of parchment paper on top of dough rectangles; top parchment with another baking sheet.
3. Bake, one pan at a time, for 15 minutes. Carefully remove top pan and parchment, and bake until deep golden brown, 3 to 5 minutes more. Let cool completely on pans on wire racks.
4. Sift confectioners' sugar onto 12 pieces of pastry as desired.
5. Transfer Vanilla Bean Crème Mousseline to a pastry bag fitted with a small round piping tip (Ateco #802). Pipe mousseline in two rows of dots onto remaining 24 pastry pieces. Stack piped pastries two layers high; top with sugar-dusted pastries. Serve immediately with berries. Best served same day as baked and assembled.

Vanilla Bean Crème Mousseline

Makes about 2½ cups

1½ cups (360 grams) whole milk
1 cup (200 grams) granulated sugar, divided
4 large egg yolks (74 grams)
¼ cup plus 1½ tablespoons (44 grams) cornstarch
¼ teaspoon kosher salt
½ cup (113 grams) plus 2 tablespoons (28 grams) unsalted butter, room temperature and divided
1½ teaspoons (9 grams) vanilla bean paste

1. In a large saucepan, heat milk and ¾ cup (150 grams) sugar over medium heat, whisking frequently, until sugar dissolves and mixture is steaming. (Do not boil.)
2. In a large bowl, whisk together egg yolks, cornstarch, salt, and remaining ¼ cup (50 grams) sugar. Gradually add warm milk mixture, whisking constantly. Return mixture to saucepan, and cook over medium heat, whisking constantly, until thickened and bubbly, 4 to 5 minutes.
3. Strain mixture through a fine-mesh sieve into a medium heatproof bowl. Whisk in 2 tablespoons (28 grams) butter and vanilla bean paste until butter is melted and mixture is smooth and well combined. Cover with plastic wrap, pressing wrap directly onto surface of pastry cream to prevent a skin from forming. Refrigerate until an instant-read thermometer registers 65°F (18°C) to 70°F (21°C), 2½ to 3 hours.
4. In the bowl of a stand mixer fitted with the paddle attachment, beat remaining ½ cup (113 grams) butter at medium speed until smooth, about 1 minute, stopping to scrape bottom and sides of bowl.
5. Whisk cold pastry cream until smooth. With mixer on medium speed, gradually add pastry cream to butter, beating until combined after each addition, stopping to scrape bottom and sides of bowl and paddle. Use immediately.

Berry Palmiers

Makes 24 palmiers

Shaped into an iconic double swirl, *palmiers* take the crown for the most delicate of French cookies. I filled these with a homemade blackberry and blueberry jam for a fruity summertime twist on the classic.

All-purpose flour, for dusting
½ recipe Classic Puff Pastry Dough (recipe on page 18)
3 tablespoons (36 grams) turbinado sugar
½ cup (148 grams) Berry Jam (recipe follows)
1 tablespoon (8 grams) cornstarch

1. On a lightly floured surface, roll Classic Puff Pastry Dough into a 12½-inch square. Sprinkle with turbinado sugar. Using a rolling pin, gently roll over sugar to press into dough. Carefully turn dough over so sugar side is down.
2. In a small bowl, stir together Berry Jam and cornstarch. Spread jam mixture onto dough. Starting from opposite sides, roll up dough into a log so each log meets in the middle. Turn log on its side on a baking sheet. (It will look similar to a capital "B.") Freeze until firm enough to slice, about 15 minutes.
3. Line several baking sheets with parchment paper.
4. Place log on its side on a cutting board. Using a serrated knife, trim ¼ inch off each end of log. Cut log into ½-inch-thick slices. Place slices, cut side up, 2 inches apart on prepared pans. Freeze until firm, 10 to 15 minutes.
5. Preheat oven to 400°F (200°C).
6. Bake until bottoms are golden brown, 15 to 20 minutes. Let cool on pans for 5 minutes. Remove from pans, and let cool completely on wire racks. Store in an airtight container for up to 2 days.

Berry Jam

Makes about 3 cups

18 ounces (510 grams) fresh blackberries (about 3½ cups)
14 ounces (397 grams) fresh blueberries (about 2⅔ cups)
2 cups (400 grams) granulated sugar
¼ cup (60 grams) almond liqueur
1 vanilla bean, split lengthwise, seeds scraped and reserved

1. In the work bowl of a food processor, process blackberries until puréed. Strain through a fine-mesh sieve into a medium bowl, discarding seeds.
2. In a larg, heavy-bottomed nonreactive saucepan, stir together 1⅔ cups (400 grams) blackberry purée, blueberries, sugar, liqueur, and vanilla bean and reserved seeds. Let stand for 30 minutes.
3. Bring berry mixture to a boil over medium heat. Cook, stirring frequently, until mixture is thickened and jam leaves a trace when a spoon is dragged across bottom of pot, 20 to 25 minutes. Remove from heat, and let cool completely. Refrigerate in an airtight container for up to 2 weeks.

Note: *Cook time for jam can vary based on the ripeness and water content of fruit; softer, riper berries will cook faster than firmer fruit.*

Guava-and-Cheese Pastelitos

Makes 12 pastries or 1 braided loaf

Creamy and crispy, buttery, and perfectly delightful, these pastelitos are as satisfying to make as they are to eat.

1 large egg (50 grams)
1 tablespoon (15 grams) water
1 (14-ounce) package (396 grams) guava paste
¾ cup (169 grams) cream cheese, room temperature
All-purpose flour, for dusting
Classic Puff Pastry Dough (recipe on page 18)
Demerara sugar, for sprinkling

1. In a small bowl, whisk together egg and 1 tablespoon (15 grams) water.
2. For triangles: Line 2 rimmed baking sheets with parchment paper. Cut guava paste into 12 pieces (1½ tablespoons or 26 grams each). Cut cream cheese into 12 pieces (1 tablespoon or 14 grams each).
3. On a lightly floured surface, roll Classic Puff Pastry Dough into an 18x14-inch rectangle (about ¼ inch thick). Using a sharp knife or a pastry wheel, trim edges of dough.
Cut dough into 12 (4½-inch) squares. Place 1 piece of guava paste in center of 1 dough square; top each with 1 piece of cream cheese. Brush edges with egg wash. Fold 1 corner of dough over filling to make a triangle, pressing dough together to seal. Place on prepared pans. Refrigerate until firm, about 30 minutes.
4. For braid: In a small microwave-safe bowl, stir and mash guava paste with a spoon until it becomes a smooth paste; heat on high in 30-second intervals as needed to soften. In another small bowl, repeat procedure with cream cheese.
5. Line a large rimmed baking sheet with parchment paper.
6. On a lightly floured surface, roll Classic Puff Pastry into an 18x15-inch rectangle (about ¼ inch thick). Using a sharp knife or a pastry wheel, trim ½ inch off all sides of dough. Transfer pastry to prepared pan. Using a bench scraper or the back of a small knife, lightly score a 15x6-inch rectangle in center of dough, leaving a 1-inch border on short sides and a 3-inch border on long sides. (Do not cut dough when scoring.) Spread cream cheese onto dough within scored rectangle. Spread guava paste onto cream cheese.
7. Cut slits at top and bottom of rectangle to fit width of filling, cutting away any excess in corners. Fold short edges over filling. Cut 1-inch-wide strips along each side of filling. Starting on left side, pull and stretch bottom strip and fold over filling, ending just below opposite bottom strip. Repeat with bottom strip on right side. Continue pattern, alternating left and right, until you reach end of braid. Trim excess dough from strips, and pinch ends into braid. (If dough is not sticking to itself, dab with a little water to help it seal.) Refrigerate until firm, about 30 minutes.
8. Preheat oven to 425°F (220°C).
9. Brush egg wash onto dough. Sprinkle with demerara sugar.
10. Bake triangles for 10 minutes. Rotate pans, cover with foil, and reduce oven temperature to 375°F (190°C). Bake until golden brown and an instant-read thermometer inserted into bottom layer of pastry (not filling) registers 205°F (96°C), 15 to 20 minutes more.
11. Bake braid for 15 minutes. Rotate pan, cover with foil, and reduce oven temperature to 375°F (190°C). Bake until golden brown and an instant-read thermometer inserted into bottom layer of pastry (not filling) registers 205°F (96°C), 30 to 35 minutes more.
12. Let cool on pans on wire racks for 10 minutes. Serve warm or at room temperature. Refrigerate in an airtight container for up to 3 days.

Shaping the Braid

In a small microwave-safe bowl, stir and mash guava paste with a spoon until it becomes a smooth paste; heat on high in 30-second intervals to soften. In another small bowl, repeat procedure with cream cheese.

TIP: The guava paste and cream cheese need to be smooth and soft enough to spread onto the dough.

On a lightly floured surface, roll Classic Puff Pastry into an 18x15-inch rectangle (about ¼ inch thick). Using a sharp knife or a pastry wheel, trim ½ inch off all sides of dough. Transfer pastry to prepared pan.

TIP: Trimming the sides gives you a squared-off edge and exposes the layers in the dough.

Using a bench scraper or the back of a small knife, lightly score a 15x6-inch rectangle in center of dough, leaving a 1-inch border on short sides and a 3-inch border on long sides. Spread cream cheese onto dough within scored rectangle. Spread guava paste onto cream cheese. Cut slits at top and bottom of rectangle to fit width of filling, cutting away any excess in corners. Fold short edges over filling. Cut 1-inch-wide strips along each side of filling. Starting on left side, pull and stretch bottom strip and fold over filling, ending just below opposite bottom strip. Repeat with bottom strip on right side. Continue pattern, alternating left and right, until you reach end of braid. Trim excess dough from strips, and pinch ends into braid. (If dough is not sticking to itself, dab with a little water to help it seal.) Refrigerate until firm, about 30 minutes.

TIP: Use the scores made in the pastry as a guide when spreading the filling. Spread the cream cheese to the scores, and as you spread the guava paste onto the cream cheese, leave a small border on the long sides.

Shaping Triangles

Line 2 rimmed baking sheets with parchment paper. Cut guava paste into 12 pieces (1½ tablespoons or 26 grams each). Cut cream cheese into 12 pieces (1 tablespoon or 14 grams each). On a lightly floured surface, roll Classic Puff Pastry into an 18x14-inch rectangle (about ¼ inch thick). Using a sharp knife or a pastry wheel, trim edges of dough. Cut dough into 12 (4½-inch) squares. Place 1 piece of guava paste in center of 1 dough square; top each with 1 piece of cream cheese. Brush edges with egg wash. Fold 1 corner of dough over filling to make a triangle, pressing dough together to seal. Place on prepared pans. Refrigerate until firm, about 30 minutes.

TIP: If you like, use the tines of a fork to help secure the seal after pressing the dough together with your fingers.

Flawless Finish

Brush egg wash onto dough. Sprinkle with demerara sugar.

TIP: Gently brush the entire surface of the pastry. The demerara sugar slightly caramelizes while the pastry bakes, creating a crunch on top.

Bake triangles until golden brown or braid until puffed and golden brown. Let cool on pans for 10 minutes. Serve warm or at room temperature. Refrigerate in an airtight container for up to 3 days.

Rough Puff Pastry Dough

For the crisp flakiness of classic puff pastry without all the work, this rough puff is for you!

- **1⅔ cups (377 grams) cold unsalted butter, cubed**
- **3 cups (375 grams) all-purpose flour, plus more for dusting**
- **1 tablespoon (9 grams) kosher salt**
- **⅔ cup (160 grams) ice water**

1. Freeze cold butter until firm, 15 to 20 minutes.
2. In the bowl of a stand mixer fitted with the paddle attachment, beat cold butter, flour, and salt at low speed just until butter is coated with flour. With mixer on low speed, add ⅔ cup (160 grams) ice water in a slow, steady stream, beating just until dough comes together, about 1 minute, stopping to scrape bottom and sides of bowl and turn dough to hydrate evenly. (There will still be large pieces of butter. It's OK if a few dry bits remain.)
3. Turn out dough onto a lightly floured surface, and roll into a 7-inch square. Wrap in plastic wrap, and refrigerate for 45 minutes to 1 hour.
4. On a lightly floured surface, roll dough into an 18x10-inch rectangle, lightly flouring surface and top of dough as needed. Fold dough in thirds like a letter. Rotate dough 90 degrees; roll into an 18x10-inch rectangle, and fold in thirds like a letter. Repeat procedure for a third and final turn. Wrap dough in plastic wrap, and refrigerate for at least 1 hour. (If, at any point, the butter is too soft after a fold, wrap in plastic wrap, and freeze until butter is firm again, checking every 5 minutes).

pro tip

To make your rough puff in a food processor: In the work bowl of a food processor, pulse flour and salt until combined. Add cold butter from freezer, and pulse just until butter is coated with flour and butter pieces are nickel-size, 2 to 3 times. Add ⅔ cup (160 grams) ice cold water, and process just until mixture starts to come together and no dry flour remains. Proceed with recipe from step 3.

Rough and Ready

Although my admiration for the art of puff is strong, I don't always have the time to pull together a classic puff pastry dough. Enter rough puff pastry dough. It's made of the same ingredients as classic puff pastry but with large pieces of butter laminated into the dough instead of entire slabs of butter, and it comes together faster than traditional puff. It doesn't bake up quite as high as classic puff, but the result is still buttery, flaky, and heavenly.

Rough Puff: The Letter Fold

On a lightly floured surface, roll dough into a 15x8-inch rectangle, lightly flouring surface and top of dough as needed.

With one short side closest to you, fold top third of dough over center third of dough, leaving bottom third exposed.

Fold bottom third of dough over top of dough, as if you were folding a letter to fit into an envelope.

Folding the dough like a letter stacks the pieces of butter within the dough. This repeated stacking creates layers of butter, allowing for the signature "puff" when the butter steams in the oven.

Blueberry-Lemon Turnovers

Makes 12 pastries

These handheld delights deliver the perfect filling-to-crust ratio as the beautifully bronzed pastry reveals the jewellike tones of blueberries perfectly melded with creamy mascarpone cheese and drizzled with a bright citrus glaze.

½ cup (113 grams) mascarpone cheese, room temperature
2 tablespoons (24 grams) granulated sugar
1 teaspoon (1 gram) lemon zest
All-purpose flour, for dusting
Rough Puff Pastry Dough (recipe on page 36)
Blueberry Filling (recipe follows)
1 large egg (50 grams)
1 tablespoon (15 grams) water
½ cup (60 grams) confectioners' sugar
2 teaspoons (10 grams) fresh lemon juice

1. Preheat oven to 400°F (200°C). Line 2 baking sheets with parchment paper.
2. In a medium bowl, whisk together mascarpone, granulated sugar, and lemon zest until smooth and well combined.
3. On lightly floured surface, roll Rough Puff Pastry Dough into a 16x12-inch rectangle. Cut 12 (4-inch) squares from dough; halve each square diagonally to make 2 triangles. Spread 2 teaspoons (8 grams) mascarpone mixture onto center of half of triangles; top each with 2 tablespoons (12 grams) Blueberry Filling. Place on prepared pans.
4. In a small bowl, whisk together egg and 1 tablespoon (15 grams) water. Using a pastry brush, brush edges of filled triangles with egg wash. Top with remaining triangles, and crimp with a fork to seal. Freeze until firm, about 15 minutes.
5. Using a small knife, cut 3 small vents in top of each pastry. Brush pastries with egg wash.
6. Bake for 10 minutes. Reduce oven temperature to 375°F (190°C), and bake until golden brown, about 15 minutes more. Let cool on pans for 10 minutes. Remove from pans, and let cool completely on a wire rack.
7. In a small bowl, whisk together confectioners' sugar and lemon juice; drizzle onto cooled pastries. Serve immediately.

Blueberry Filling

Makes about 1¾ cups

2½ cups (320 grams) fresh blueberries
¾ cup (150 grams) granulated sugar
2 tablespoons (16 grams) cornstarch
2 tablespoons (30 grams) fresh lemon juice
1 teaspoon (4 grams) vanilla extract
¼ teaspoon kosher salt

1. In a medium saucepan, stir together all ingredients; cook over medium-high heat, stirring occasionally, until blueberries begin to break down and mixture begins to boil. Reduce heat to medium-low; cook, stirring occasionally, until thickened, about 5 minutes. Remove from heat, and let cool completely. Refrigerate in an airtight container for up to 1 week.

Cream Horns

Makes 12 pastries

These beauties are surprisingly simple to make and irresistibly alluring with their vanilla seed-flecked snow-white cream swathed in a gloriously golden shell of pastry.

All-purpose flour, for dusting
Rough Puff Pastry Dough (recipe on page 36)
1 large egg (50 grams)
1 tablespoon (15 grams) water
¼ cup (50 grams) granulated sugar
4 ounces (113 grams) cream cheese, softened
½ cup (60 grams) confectioners' sugar
1 teaspoon (6 grams) vanilla bean paste
1 cup (240 grams) cold heavy whipping cream

1. Preheat oven to 400°F (200°C). Line 2 baking sheets with parchment paper.
2. On a lightly floured surface, roll Rough Puff Pastry Dough into a 15x13-inch rectangle. Trim ½ inch from each side. Cut rectangle into 12 (1-inch-wide) strips.
3. Starting at pointed end of a 4½- to 5-inch cream horn mold, wrap 1 strip of dough around mold, slightly overlapping pastry. Place on a prepared pan, and repeat with remaining strips. Refrigerate until firm, about 15 minutes.
4. In a small bowl, whisk together egg and 1 tablespoon (15 grams) water. Using a pastry brush, brush outside of each pastry with egg wash; sprinkle with granulated sugar.
5. Bake until puffed and golden brown, 10 to 15 minutes, rotating pans halfway through baking. Let cool on pans for 10 minutes. Remove from pans, and let cool completely on a wire rack. Carefully remove cooled pastries from molds.
6. In the bowl of a stand mixer fitted with the whisk attachment, beat cream cheese, confectioners' sugar, and vanilla bean paste at medium speed until smooth and creamy, about 2 minutes, stopping to scrape sides of bowl. With mixer on medium-high speed, add cold cream in a slow, steady stream, beating until soft peaks form and stopping to scrape bottom and sides of bowl. Beat until stiff peaks form, 2 to 3 minutes.
7. Spoon mixture into a pastry bag fitted with a small closed star piping tip (Ateco #842). Slowly pipe mixture into horns. Best served same day as filled.

pro tips

When shaping the horns, be sure to place the pastry seam side down so it keeps its shape while baking.

I recommend using cream horn molds and a pastry bag, but you can also wrap waffle cones in foil for the molds and pipe cream into the horns using a plastic bag with one of the corners snipped off.

Crème Brûlée Tarts

Makes 12 tarts

I took inspiration from French pastry chef Cedric Grolet to create these demure tarts. Bite-size and deliciously swoon-worthy, they feature a smooth vanilla-specked custard inside and crispy, flaky, buttery puff pastry shell on the outside. Their crowning glory is a crackling burnt-sugar top that shatters satisfyingly.

All-purpose flour, for dusting
Rough Puff Pastry Dough (recipe on page 36)
1 large egg white (30 grams), lightly beaten
½ cup (100 grams) granulated sugar, divided
4 large egg yolks (74 grams), room temperature
¼ teaspoon kosher salt
1 cup (240 grams) heavy whipping cream
1½ teaspoons (9 grams) vanilla bean paste

1. Preheat oven to 400°F (200°C). Line 2 baking sheets with parchment paper.
2. On a lightly floured surface, roll Rough Puff Pastry Dough into a 16x12-inch rectangle. Using a 4-inch round cutter, cut 12 rounds, and transfer each to a 3½-inch round fluted removable-bottom tart pan or mini brioche pan, pressing into bottom and up sides. Dock bottoms with a fork. Top each with a piece of parchment paper. Add pie weights.
3. Bake until edges are golden, about 15 minutes. Carefully remove parchment and weights. Press down any pastry that has puffed up unevenly, and brush inside of pastry with egg white. Bake until pastry is fully set and golden, 5 to 10 minutes more. Lightly press down any bubble that may have formed in center. Let cool completely in pans on wire racks. Gently remove tart shells from pans.
4. In a medium bowl, whisk together ¼ cup (50 grams) sugar, egg yolks, and salt.
5. In a small saucepan, heat cream and vanilla bean paste over medium-low heat, stirring frequently, just until steaming. (Do not boil.) Slowly add half of cream mixture to sugar mixture, whisking constantly. Add sugar mixture to remaining cream mixture in pan. Bring to a boil over medium heat, whisking constantly; cook until thickened and an instant-read thermometer registers 175°F (80°C), 1 to 2 minutes. Remove from heat. Divide custard among prepared tart shells (about 1½ tablespoons or 25 grams each). Refrigerate until custard is set, at least 1 hour.
6. Just before serving, sprinkle remaining ¼ cup (50 grams) sugar onto tarts. Using a small handheld kitchen torch, carefully brown sugar. Serve immediately.

pro tip

If you don't have small tart pans or mini brioche pans, you can also use a jumbo muffin pan. Use a 4½-inch round cutter and bake as directed.

Quick Kouign Amann

Makes 12 pastries

Kouign amann, a pastry from the Brittany region of France, is all about the crisp, flaky pastry and the flavor of both the caramelized sugar and the salted butter. It has a reputation for being finnicky and labor-intensive, but this recipe is a speedy yet no less tasty version.

---

3 cups (375 grams) all-purpose flour, plus more for dusting
1¾ cups (396 grams) cold salted butter, cubed
2 teaspoons (6 grams) kosher salt
⅔ cup (160 grams) ice water
1 cup (200 grams) granulated sugar, divided, plus more for sprinkling
½ cup (160 grams) cherry preserves (optional)
½ cup (128 grams) hazelnut-chocolate spread (optional)

1. In the bowl of a stand mixer fitted with the paddle attachment, beat flour, cold butter, and salt at low speed just until butter is coated with flour. With mixer on low speed, add ⅔ cup (160 grams) ice water in a slow, steady stream, beating just until dough comes together, about 1 minute, stopping to scrape bottom and sides of bowl and turn dough to hydrate evenly. (There will still be large pieces of butter. It is OK if a few dry bits remain).
2. Turn out dough onto a lightly floured surface, and roll into a 9-inch square. Wrap in plastic wrap, and refrigerate for 45 minutes to 1 hour.
3. On a lightly floured surface, roll dough into an 18x10-inch rectangle, lightly flouring surface and top of dough as needed. Fold dough in thirds like a letter. Rotate dough 90 degrees; roll into an 18x10-inch rectangle, and spread ¼ cup (50 grams) sugar over center third of rectangle. Fold in thirds like a letter. Repeat procedure for a third and final turn, spreading ¼ cup (50 grams) sugar over center third of rectangle. Wrap dough in plastic wrap, and refrigerate for at least 1 hour. (See Pro Tips.)
4. Preheat oven to 375°F (190°C). Spray a 12-cup muffin pan with baking spray with flour. Sprinkle 1 teaspoon (4 grams) sugar in bottom of each cup.
5. Lightly sprinkle sugar onto work surface. Turn out dough onto surface, and roll into a 16x12-inch rectangle. Sprinkle sugar onto dough, lightly pressing with your hands to adhere. Cut 12 (4-inch) squares from dough. Fold corners of 1 square into center. Gather sides toward center, and place in a prepared muffin cup. Repeat with remaining pastry squares. Sprinkle remaining ¼ cup (50 grams) sugar onto pastries.
6. Bake until golden brown, 35 to 45 minutes. Immediately remove from pan, and let cool completely on a wire rack.
7. Fill pastries, if desired. Using a small knife, cut a hole in center of each pastry. Spoon preserves and hazelnut-chocolate spread into individual pastry bags fitted with a small round piping tip. Pipe into pastries as desired. Serve filled pastries immediately. Store unfilled pastries in an airtight container for up to 3 days.

pro tips

If your kitchen is hot (especially during summer months), the butter and sugar can melt quickly during lamination. If, at any point, the dough feels too soft to handle, wrap it in plastic wrap and refrigerate for 15 to 20 minutes between folds.

Refrigerating the dough for long periods of time will cause the sugar to liquify, so the dough is best baked the same day it's made.

Avoid using a dark muffin pan, if possible, as it will caramelize the sugar on the outside before the pastry is fully baked through.

Shaping Kouign Amann

Working with one piece of pastry at a time, fold two opposite corners of the pastry into the center so the corners meet.

Next, fold in a third corner, gently pressing with your fingertip so the corners stay in place. Gently flare out the two curved sides of the dough using your thumb and index finger.

Fold in the last corner to the center, gently pressing so all corners now meet. Repeat flaring out all the curved sides of the pastry.

Gently press and squeeze all the corners in toward the center. Gently lift the shaped pastry, and place in a muffin cup.

Chaussons aux Pommes

Makes 15 pastries

These French apple turnovers marry two fall favorites—apples and spice—in a buttery pocket of flaky pastry. A blend of four spices, *quatre épices* in French, is added to the filling for a peppery sweet bite, complementing the fresh, tangy flavor of apple and bright notes of citrus.

All-purpose flour, for dusting
Rough Puff Pastry Dough (recipe on page 36)
3 tablespoons (45 grams) water, divided
2 large egg yolks (37 grams)
Apple Filling (recipe follows)
2 tablespoons (24 grams) granulated sugar

1. Preheat oven to 400°F (200°C). Line a baking sheet with parchment paper.
2. On a lightly floured surface, roll Rough Puff Pastry Dough into a 21x13-inch rectangle (about ⅛ inch thick). Using a 4-inch round fluted cutter, cut out 15 circles, making sure to cut closely to previous cut. Discard scraps. Gently roll and stretch circles into 5½x4-inch ovals. Place on prepared pan. (Cover first layer with parchment paper, and stack a second layer on top; no need to use a second pan.) Freeze until dough is firm, about 5 minutes.
3. In a small bowl, whisk together 1 tablespoon (15 grams) water and egg yolks. Brush ovals with egg wash. Divide Apple Filling (about 1 tablespoon or 19 grams each) among pastry ovals. Fold ovals in half, creating a pocket, gently pressing together edges to seal. Return to pan. Brush tops with egg wash, and freeze until egg wash is set, about 5 minutes. Brush with egg wash again; freeze for 5 minutes more.
4. In a small microwave-safe bowl, heat sugar and remaining 2 tablespoons (30 grams) water on high until sugar dissolves, about 30 seconds, stirring as needed.
5. Line a baking sheet with parchment paper. Place half of pastries on prepared pan; return remaining pan of pastries to freezer. Using a small sharp knife, gently score desired design into top of pastries. Using a wooden pick, poke 4 to 5 holes in pastry to vent.
6. Bake until pastry is puffed and golden brown, about 20 minutes, rotating pan halfway through baking. Brush with simple syrup, and bake until deep golden brown and top of pastry looks dry and shiny, 1 to 3 minutes more. Let cool on pan on a wire rack for at least 15 minutes. Repeat with remaining pastries. Serve warm or at room temperature. Best served same day.

Apple Filling

Makes 1¼ cups

2 cups (280 grams) ¾- to 1-inch-chopped peeled Granny Smith apples (about 3 small apples)
2 tablespoons (24 grams) granulated sugar
¼ teaspoon orange zest
2 tablespoons (30 grams) fresh orange juice
1 teaspoon (2 grams) Quatre Épices Spice Mix (recipe follows)
3 tablespoons (24 grams) golden raisins
½ teaspoon (2 grams) vanilla extract

1. In a medium saucepan, combine apples, sugar, orange zest and juice, and Quatre Épices Spice Mix. Bring to a boil over medium-high heat, stirring frequently. Cover and reduce heat to medium-low; cook, stirring frequently, until apples are softened, about 10 minutes. Remove from heat; using a potato masher or a fork, roughly mash apples until pieces are about ¼ inch. Stir in raisins and vanilla. Let cool completely before using.

Quatre Épices Spice Mix

Makes about ½ cup

3 tablespoons (18 grams) ground white pepper
1½ tablespoons (9 grams) ground ginger
1½ tablespoons (9 grams) ground nutmeg
1½ tablespoons (9 grams) ground cloves

1. In a small resealable jar, shake together all ingredients. Store for up to 1 year.

Hazelnut-Chocolate Bear Claws

Makes 6 pastries

Traditionally made from a yeast-leavened Danish pastry dough, baking bear claws could be an all-day affair. But with quick rough puff pastry, you can still get all the flakiness you love but with no rise time and extra-fast lamination. Chocolate and hazelnut come together to make a rich and nutty filling. A final sprinkling of pearl sugar and these homemade bear claws will take hold of your taste buds.

All-purpose flour, for dusting
Hazelnut-Chocolate Filling (recipe follows)
Rough Puff Pastry Dough (recipe on page 36)
1 large egg (50 grams), lightly beaten
Swedish pearl sugar, for sprinkling

1. Line 2 rimmed baking sheets with parchment paper.
2. Divide Hazelnut-Chocolate Filling into 6 portions (about 2 tablespoons or 34 grams each), and place on a prepared pan; shape each portion into a 3¼x1¾-inch rectangle, and cover with plastic wrap.
3. On a lightly floured surface, roll dough into a 16x11½-inch rectangle. Trim edges to create a 15x11-inch rectangle. Cut rectangle in half lengthwise to create 2 (15x5½-inch) rectangles; cut each half into 3 (5½x5-inch) rectangles.
4. Position 1 dough rectangle with a 5-inch side closest to you. Place 1 filling rectangle on lower half of rectangle, leaving a ¾-inch border. Brush all edges of dough with egg; fold dough over filling to make 5-inch sides meet, firmly pressing edges to seal. Using a pastry cutter or pastry wheel, trim ⅟₁₆- to ⅛-inch of dough off sealed edges to further seal. Using a paring knife, make 4 (¾-inch-long) equally spaced cuts along the long sealed edge of dough, being careful not to cut through to filling. Repeat procedure with remaining dough rectangles and remaining filling. Place at least 1 inch apart on remaining prepared pan, gently curving to spread out cuts. Freeze for 10 minutes.
5. Preheat oven to 400°F (200°C).
6. Brush egg onto dough; sprinkle with pearl sugar.
7. Bake for 15 minutes. Reduce oven temperature to 375°F (190°C), and bake until puffed and golden brown, about 10 minutes. Let cool on pans for 15 minutes.

Hazelnut-Chocolate Filling

Makes ⅔ cup

½ cup (48 grams) finely ground hazelnut flour
3 tablespoons (21 grams) confectioners' sugar
⅛ teaspoon kosher salt
⅓ cup (92 grams) hazelnut-chocolate spread
1 large egg yolk (19 grams), room temperature
2 tablespoons (28 grams) unsalted butter, melted

1. In a medium bowl, stir together flour, confectioners' sugar, and salt. Add hazelnut-chocolate spread, egg yolk, and melted butter; stir until well combined, kneading together by hand toward end if needed. (Mixture will be quite thick.) Use immediately.

Pâte Feuilletée:
PUFF PASTRY DOUGH

Mini Galettes des Rois

Makes 5 (4-inch) galettes

The *galette des rois*, or French king cake, is traditionally made to celebrate the Christian feast day of Epiphany on January 6, which commemorates the day the three kings arrived to visit the infant Jesus. Combining easy rough puff pastry, a simple almond filling, and an eye-catching pattern, these beauties will make you the reigning royal of dessert.

---

3 tablespoons (42 grams) unsalted butter, room temperature
½ cup (48 grams) superfine natural almond flour
¼ cup (50 grams) granulated sugar
2 large egg yolks (38 grams), divided
1½ teaspoons (4.5 grams) all-purpose flour, plus more for dusting
¼ teaspoon (1 gram) almond extract
⅛ teaspoon kosher salt
Rough Puff Pastry Dough (recipe on page 36)
1 whole almond (optional)
1 teaspoon (5 grams) water, plus more for brushing

1. In a small bowl, stir butter until creamy. Stir in almond flour, sugar, 1 egg yolk (19 grams), all-purpose flour, extract, and salt until well combined.
2. Line 2 baking sheets with parchment paper.
3. Divide Rough Puff Pastry Dough in half. Lightly dust a work surface with all-purpose flour. On prepared surface, roll one portion of dough into a 12x9-inch rectangle (about ⅛ inch thick). Using a 4-inch round cutter, cut 5 circles. Place 2 inches apart on a prepared pan. Repeat procedure with remaining dough.
4. Using the tines of a fork, prick 5 dough circles several times to dock. Spread 2 tablespoons (about 30 grams) almond flour mixture on each docked circle, leaving a ½- to ¾-inch border around edges. Place whole almond (if using) in almond flour mixture on 1 circle.
5. Lightly brush water onto edges of dough. Top with remaining dough circles, lining up edges and pressing down to seal with bottom circles. Refrigerate for 30 minutes.
6. Preheat oven to 400°F (200°C).
7. Using your fingertip, press down dough edge; using the back of a small knife, simultaneously make a notch just to the side of your fingertip as if marking its location. Move fingertip to other side of notch, and make another notch. Repeat procedure all around edge and with remaining galettes. Score desired design on top of each galette.
8. In another small bowl, whisk together 1 teaspoon (5 grams) water and remaining 1 egg yolk (19 grams). Brush on top crust, being careful not to let egg drip down sides. Cut 5 small slits in top crust to let steam escape.
9. Bake for 15 minutes. Rotate pans, reduce oven temperature to 375°F (190°C), and bake until golden brown, 10 to 15 minutes more, re-opening slits in tops if needed. Serve warm, or let cool completely on a wire rack. Store in an airtight container for up to 2 days.

pro tip

In France, it's tradition to bake a *fève* (bean) into the galette. The lucky guest who finds the fève in their slice gets to be *roi* (king) for the day. Today's fèves include a range of trinkets and figurines of various sizes, shapes, and materials. I like to use an edible, affordable whole almond, but feel free to substitute another favorite nut or piece of dried fruit.

Scalloped and Scored

To create a traditional scalloped edge, using your fingertip, press down dough edge; using the back of a small knife, simultaneously make a notch just to the side of your fingertip as if marking its location. Move fingertip to other side of notch, and repeat all the way around.

Using a small knife, score 3 evenly spaced, parallel lines across top to create 4 columns. (Be careful not to cut through pastry.) Score evenly spaced diagonal lines all the way down one column.

In adjacent column, score diagonal lines that mirror your first set to create a slight "V" shape. Repeat procedure in outer columns, only scoring up to ¼ inch from dough edges. (The "V" shape will be reversed.) Brush tops with egg wash, being careful not to let egg wash drip down sides. Cut slits in scored design to let steam escape.

pâte friable

pie and tart crust dough

TARTE AU CITRON, LINZER TORTE, FRANGIPANE TART

Pâte friable, or "crumbly dough," can be further categorized as *pâte brisée* ("broken"), *pâte sablée* ("sandy"), and *pâte sucrée* ("sweet"). Yet no matter the style of pâte friable, each is comprised of at least flour, fat, salt, and water or another liquid or dairy for moisture.

Pâte Brisée

Brisée is the French term for "broken," referencing the broken pieces of butter in this shortcrust dough. Pâte brisée is traditionally mixed by *frissage,* using the heel of your hand to rub and smear butter pieces into the dough. This also creates a tender texture because the fat is more thoroughly worked into the dough. The movement of a stand mixer with a paddle attachment imitates the frissage motion.

1½ cups (188 grams) all-purpose flour
1½ teaspoons (6 grams) granulated sugar
½ teaspoon (1.5 grams) kosher salt
½ cup (113 grams) cold unsalted butter, cubed
¼ cup (60 grams) ice water

1. In the bowl of a stand mixer fitted with the paddle attachment, beat flour, sugar, and salt at low speed until combined. Add cold butter, and beat at medium-low speed until mixture is crumbly.
2. With mixer on medium-low speed, add ¼ cup (60 grams) ice water, beating until dough comes together.
3. Turn out dough, and shape into a disk. Wrap tightly in plastic wrap, and refrigerate for at least 30 minutes or up to 3 days or freeze for up to 2 months. Let frozen dough thaw overnight in refrigerator before using. If refrigerating dough for longer than 30 minutes, let it stand at room temperature for 10 minutes before rolling out.

Pâte Sablée

Sablée, or "sandy" describes how the texture and consistency of this dough should be once the fat and flour have been properly worked together. *Pâte sablée* has a lighter, more crubly texture than *pâte brisée* or *pâte sucrée.*

---

2 cups (250 grams) all-purpose flour
½ cup (60 grams) confectioners' sugar
½ teaspoon (1.5 grams) kosher salt
½ cup (113 grams) cold unsalted butter, cubed
1 large egg (50 grams), lightly beaten

1. In a large bowl, whisk together flour, confectioners' sugar, and salt. Using a pastry blender or your hands, cut in cold butter until mixture resembles coarse meal. Add egg, and stir until combined.
2. Turn out dough, and press firmly with your hands until dough comes together and is fully hydrated, being careful not to knead too much. Shape dough into a disk, and wrap in plastic wrap. Refrigerate for at least 30 minutes or up to 3 days or freeze for up to 2 months. Let frozen dough thaw overnight in refrigerator before using. If refrigerating the dough for longer than 30 minutes, let it stand at room temperature for 10 minutes before rolling out.

Pâte Sucrée

Sucrée, French for "sweet," and this style of shortcrust often contains more sugar or other sweetener as compared to other pâte friables; however, *pâte sucrée*'s defining characteristic is that the fat and sugar are whipped or beaten together into a paste before adding flour, which results in a crisp, sturdy cookie-like crust.

½ cup (113 grams) unsalted butter, softened
⅓ cup (80 grams) confectioners' sugar
½ teaspoon (1.5 grams) kosher salt
1 large egg (50 grams), room temperature
2 cups (250 grams) all-purpose flour

1. In the bowl of a stand mixer fitted with the paddle attachment, beat butter, confectioners' sugar, and salt at medium speed until pale and creamy, 2 to 3 minutes. Add egg, and beat until combined, stopping to scrape sides and bottom of bowl. With mixer on low speed, gradually add flour, beating until just combined.

2. Turn out dough, and shape into a disk. Wrap in plastic wrap, and refrigerate for at least 30 minutes or up to 3 days or freeze for up to 2 months. Let frozen dough thaw overnight in refrigerator before using. If refrigerating the dough for longer than 30 minutes, let it stand at room temperature for 10 minutes before rolling out.

Pâte Down Pat

The three pâte friables can be remembered by:

BRoken for **BR**isée
SAndy for **SA**blée
SUgar for **SU**crée

No matter which of the three pâte friables you choose to make, the resulting character of your pastry depends on how you incorporate the fat with the flour. The key to a flaky crust is minimal mixing once the butter has been cut in to keep tiny, whole pieces of fat that are evenly dispersed throughout the dough. As the butter melts in the oven, it gives off water that turns to steam. The super-heated steam puffs up and separates the layers of dough. Whether you mix your dough by hand or in a food processor, the goal is to surround small bits of fat with flour and keep it cold.

Cold ingredients and limited handling create the best crust, so it's important to be methodical when getting your dough ready to bake. When rolling out your dough, using a long rolling pin is best. Be careful not to use too much flour when rolling, or your crust can be tough.

Make Your Dough

Pâte friable can be made by hand or in a food processor, depending on the specific type of dough. Using a food processor is more efficient and also keeps the ingredients colder, which results in a flakier crust. However, mixing by hand allows you to monitor the size of the butter pieces in the flour.

By Hand

Whisk together dry ingredients in a large bowl. Using a pastry blender or your hands, cut cold butter into flour mixture.

A pastry blender limits the amount of contact with your warm hands, but you'll know exactly when to stop working in the butter if you use your hands.

Add your liquid ingredients, and use your fingers to stir, toss, and massage mixture until it comes together and forms a dough.

In a Food Processor

This is how your dough will look once made in a food processor. The dough may look crumbly, but it should be moist—but not sticky—and hold together when gently squeezed.

Pick Your Pan

When choosing a pie or tart pan, the most important thing to remember is that your crust needs to cook fast. All shape will be lost if the fat melts before the protein structure starts to set.

GLASS PANS conduct heat evenly, giving your crust the most thorough bake. While other materials bake by heat conduction only, glass bakes by both conduction and radiant heat energy. This allows the heat to go directly through glass to the crust.

CERAMIC PANS are the most decorative and also conduct heat fairly evenly, but unlike glass, you can't see through them to determine if your crust is done.

METAL PANS brown crust more quickly because they become hotter in the oven. Dark or dull metal pans are preferred because they absorb heat and bake faster than shiny pans. Heavier metal pans made of a good heat conductor, like aluminum, give you a more evenly baked crust than thinner, less conductive metal like tin.

Rolling Out Your Crust

Follow these steps to get your pâte friables from dough disk to pan quickly and easily

Roll chilled dough from center outward using firm (but not hard) and steady pressure. Avoid pressing down on edges so they don't become too thin. Give the dough a quarter turn, and roll again. Lightly flour underneath dough as necessary to prevent sticking. If dough becomes too soft or warm, return it to the refrigerator for 5 to 10 minutes before working again. Repeat rolling and turning steps until dough is wide enough to overhang the pie plate by 1 to 2 inches. For a 9-inch pie plate, roll the crust to 12 inches.

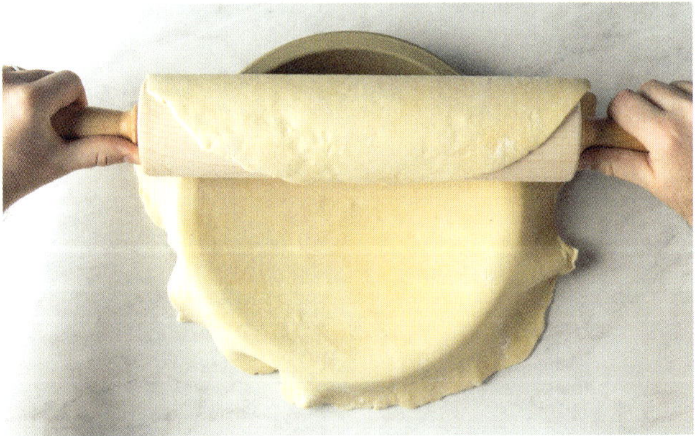

To transfer dough to plate, place pin about 2 inches from top of rolled-out dough circle. Fold top edge of dough over rolling pin, and turn once to loosely roll around pin. Lift the pin, and carefully move to middle of the plate and unfold dough.

Let the dough fall into the pan as you unroll it off the pin. Gently lift the dough around the edges and let it drape all the way down the sides of the pan and into the bottom.

Gently press the dough into place. Avoid stretching the dough, as it will just shrink back during baking. Trim the excess dough to ½ to 1 inch past the edge of the pan, fold edges under, and crimp as desired.

Parbaking and Blind Baking

Although these terms often get used interchangeably, there is a distinct difference between them

As the word indicates, parbaking a piecrust means to bake it partially. **Parbaking** is standard practice for many pies with juicy or liquid-y fillings such as fresh fruit, pumpkin, and quiche. **Blind baking** takes parbaking a step further, fully baking the empty piecrust until it's golden brown and set throughout. Blind-baked crusts are used with no-bake fillings like a cooked custard or pudding. Why would you want to parbake or blind-bake your piecrust? Doing so gives the piecrust a head start on baking so it stays crisp and firm rather than soft and soggy, and it prevents your filling from overbaking.

Line your piecrust with a piece of parchment paper large enough to extend over the sides of the crust so that you can seccurely pick up the parchment. (You can also use heavy-duty foil instead of parchment.) Fill the parchment two-thirds to three-fourths full with pie weights and spread them in an even layer.

Bake the crust according to your recipe or until the edges of the crust look dry and are beginning to turn very lightly brown.

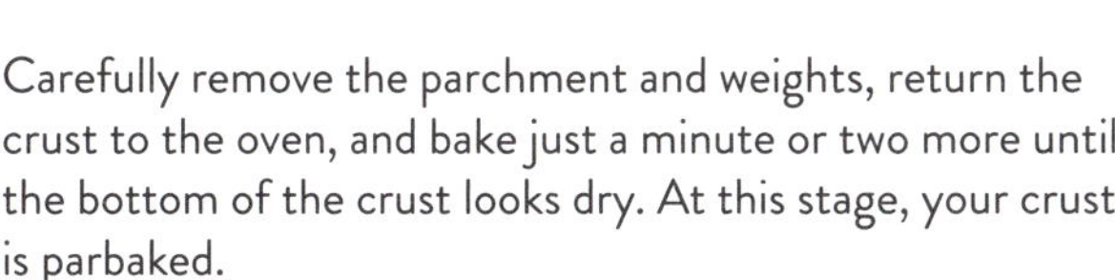

Carefully remove the parchment and weights, return the crust to the oven, and bake just a minute or two more until the bottom of the crust looks dry. At this stage, your crust is parbaked.

For a blind-baked crust, continue baking the crust until it's golden brown and crisp all over. You may need to cover the edges of the crust with foil to prevent them from overbrowning while the sides and bottom of the crust set. Let your blind-baked crust cool completely before filling it.

Honey-Nut Pie

Makes 1 (9-inch) pie

If you like a pie with crunch, this is the recipe for you. I updated classic pecan pie with a unique blend of hazelnuts, pecans, pine nuts, and walnuts enveloped by a floral orange blossom honey batter held in a tender Pâte Brisée crust.

All-purpose flour, for dusting
Pâte Brisée (recipe on page 56)
½ cup (100 grams) granulated sugar
⅓ cup (113 grams) orange blossom honey
¼ cup (85 grams) light corn syrup
1 teaspoon (3 grams) kosher salt
¾ cup (170 grams) unsalted butter, cubed
½ cup (120 grams) heavy whipping cream
1 large egg (50 grams)
1 large egg yolk (19 grams)
½ cup (57 grams) pine nuts
½ cup (57 grams) chopped pecans
½ cup (57 grams) chopped walnuts
½ cup (57 grams) chopped hazelnuts

1. On a lightly floured surface, roll Pâte Brisée into a 12-inch circle. Transfer to a 9-inch pie plate, pressing into bottom and up sides. Trim dough to ½ inch beyond edge of plate. Fold edges under, and crimp as desired. Freeze for 20 minutes.
2. Preheat oven to 350°F (180°C).
3. Top dough with a piece of parchment paper, letting ends extend over edges of plate. Add pie weights.
4. Bake until edges are set and golden brown, about 12 minutes. Carefully remove parchment and weights. Bake 8 minutes more. Leave oven on.
5. In a medium saucepan, bring sugar, honey, corn syrup, and salt to a boil over medium heat, whisking until sugar dissolves. Whisk in butter until melted and smooth. Pour into a large heatproof bowl, and let cool for 30 minutes.
6. Whisk cream, egg, and egg yolk into honey mixture. Sprinkle nuts in bottom of prepared crust. Pour honey mixture onto nuts.
7. Bake until crust is golden brown and center is set, 50 minutes to 1 hour, covering crust with foil to prevent excess browning, if necessary. Let cool completely on a wire rack before serving. Store in an airtight container for up to 3 days.

Parisian Flan

Makes 1 (9-inch) flan

With a velvety custard filling, a flaky citrus-infused pâte brisée crust, and a splash of orange liqueur, this flan is authentically Parisian. It's important to cover the crust during the last few minutes of baking so you get a beautifully browned top without burning the crust. Let the flan refrigerate overnight so it achieves the subtle jiggle it's famous for.

3¾ cups (900 grams) whole milk
1¼ cups (300 grams) heavy whipping cream
1¼ cups (250 grams) granulated sugar, divided
1 vanilla bean, split lengthwise, seeds scraped and reserved
5 large eggs (250 grams)
1 large egg yolk (19 grams)
½ cup (64 grams) cornstarch
2 tablespoons (30 grams) orange liqueur
Orange Pâte Brisée (recipe follows)
All-purpose flour, for dusting
2 tablespoons (40 grams) apricot jam, warmed and strained
1 teaspoon (5 grams) water

1. In a large saucepan, heat milk, cream, ¼ cup (50 grams) sugar, vanilla bean, and reserved seeds over medium heat, whisking frequently, until steaming and an instant-read thermometer registers 180°F (82°C).
2. In a large bowl, whisk together eggs, egg yolk, cornstarch, and remaining 1 cup (200 grams) sugar until smooth. Slowly add hot milk mixture, whisking constantly. Pour egg mixture into saucepan, and cook over medium heat, whisking constantly, until mixture is thickened and registers 185°F (85°C) on an instant-read thermometer, 5 to 8 minutes.
3. Strain mixture through a fine-mesh sieve into a large bowl, discarding solids; whisk in liqueur. Cover with plastic wrap, pressing wrap directly onto surface of custard to prevent a skin from forming. Refrigerate until cold, 3 to 4 hours.
4. Lightly butter a 9-inch springform pan. Line bottom of pan with parchment paper.
5. Let Orange Pâte Brisée stand at room temperature for 10 minutes. On a lightly floured surface, roll Pâte Brisée into a 14-inch circle. Transfer to prepared pan, pressing into bottom and up sides. Freeze for 15 minutes.
6. Preheat oven to 375°F (190°C).
7. Trim dough to a height of 2 inches inside of pan. Pour custard into prepared crust, smoothing top with an offset spatula.
8. Bake until crust is golden brown and top of custard jiggles slightly when pan is gently shaken, 40 to 45 minutes. Remove flan from oven, and increase oven temperature to broil.
9. Cover crust with foil, pressing foil down into pan to reach crust. (Custard should remain exposed.) Return flan to oven, and broil for 2 to 3 minutes, depending on desired level of char. Let cool completely in pan on a wire rack. Refrigerate overnight.
10. Just before serving, whisk together jam and 1 teaspoon (5 grams) water; brush onto flan. Serve immediately.

Orange Pâte Brisée

Makes 1 (9-inch) deep-dish crust

2 cups (250 grams) all-purpose flour
1 tablespoon (12 grams) granulated sugar
1 tablespoon (11 grams) packed orange zest (about 2 large oranges)
½ teaspoon (1.5 grams) kosher salt
¾ cup (113 grams) cold unsalted butter, cubed
¼ cup (60 grams) whole milk
1 large egg yolk (19 grams)

1. In the bowl of a stand mixer fitted with the paddle attachment, beat flour, sugar, orange zest, and salt at low speed until combined. Add cold butter, and beat at medium-low speed until mixture is crumbly.
2. In a small bowl, whisk together milk and egg yolk. With mixer on medium-low speed, add milk mixture to flour mixture, beating until dough comes together.
3. Turn out dough, and shape into a disk. Wrap in plastic wrap, and refrigerate until firm, about 2 hours.

Blackberry-Nectarine Frangipane Tart

Makes 1 (9-inch) tart

Layered with juicy berries and tangy stone fruit, this confection is as stunning as it is tasty. Each indulgent slice is held together in a delicate, crumbly Pâte Sablée and filled with a creamy almond frangipane. With a dessert this bright and beautiful, your summertime celebrations are sure to shine!

---

2 tablespoons (16 grams) all-purpose flour, plus more for dusting
Pâte Sablée (recipe on page 58)
½ cup (113 grams) unsalted butter, room temperature
½ cup (100 grams) granulated sugar
2 large eggs (100 grams), room temperature
1 cup (96 grams) almond flour
2 teaspoons (8 grams) vanilla extract
½ teaspoon (1.5 grams) kosher salt
¼ teaspoon (1 gram) almond extract
1 medium nectarine (170 grams), halved, pitted, and cut into ½-inch-thick slices
½ cup (80 grams) fresh blackberries
2 tablespoons (40 grams) apricot jam, warmed

1. On a lightly floured surface, roll Pâte Sablée into a 12-inch circle (about ⅛ inch thick). Carefully transfer to a 9-inch round fluted removable-bottom tart pan, lightly pressing into bottom and up sides. Using a paring knife, trim excess dough. Prick bottom of dough all over with a fork. Refrigerate until firm, at least 30 minutes.
2. Preheat oven to 325°F (170°C).
3. Top dough with a piece of parchment paper, letting ends extend over edges of pan. Add pie weights.
4. Bake until edges are set, about 15 minutes. Carefully remove parchment and weights. Bake until surface is dry and lightly browned, about 10 minutes more. Let cool completely in pan. Increase oven temperature to 375°F (190°C).
5. In the bowl of a stand mixer fitted with the paddle attachment, beat butter and sugar at medium speed until light and creamy, 2 to 3 minutes, stopping to scrape sides of bowl. Add eggs, one at a time, beating well after each addition and stopping to scrape sides of bowl. With mixer on low speed, gradually add almond flour and all-purpose flour, beating until just combined. Beat in vanilla, salt, and almond extract. Spread mixture into cooled prepared crust. Top with nectarines and blackberries as desired.
6. Bake until center is set and top is golden brown, about 30 minutes, covering with foil during final 10 minutes of baking to prevent excess browning. Let cool in pan for 10 minutes. Remove from pan, and place on a wire rack.
7. Gently brush jam onto fruit in warm tart. Let cool completely before serving. Refrigerate in an airtight container for up to 3 days.

Cherry-Almond Bakewell Tart

Makes 1 (9-inch) tart

A Bakewell tart is a classic British dessert named after the Derbyshire town of Bakewell. This irresistible treat is traditionally made with raspberry jam, but I love using tart cherry preserves to complement the frangipane—a rich almond filling—and the buttery, tender crust. A scattering of sliced almonds on top and a simple glaze add sweetness and crunch.

2 tablespoons (16 grams) all-purpose flour, plus more for dusting
Pâte Sucrée (recipe on page 60)
1 large egg white (30 grams), lightly beaten
½ cup (113 grams) unsalted butter, room temperature
½ cup (100 grams) granulated sugar
2 large eggs (100 grams), room temperature
2 teaspoons (8 grams) vanilla extract
½ teaspoon (1.5 grams) kosher salt
¼ teaspoon (1 gram) almond extract
1 cup (96 grams) almond flour
¾ cup (240 grams) cherry preserves
¼ cup (28 grams) sliced almonds
½ cup (60 grams) confectioners' sugar
1 tablespoon (15 grams) whole milk

1. On a lightly floured surface, roll Pâte Sucrée to a 12-inch circle (about ⅛ inch thick). Carefully transfer to a 9-inch round fluted removable-bottom tart pan, lightly pressing into bottom and up sides. Using a paring knife, trim excess dough. Prick bottom of dough all over with a fork. Refrigerate until firm, at least 30 minutes.
2. Preheat oven to 325°F (170°C).
3. Top dough with a piece of parchment paper, letting ends extend over edges of pan. Add pie weights.
4. Bake until edges are set, about 15 minutes. Carefully remove parchment and weights, and brush bottom of crust with egg white.
5. Bake until surface of crust is dry and lightly browned, about 15 minutes more. Let cool completely in pan. Increase oven temperature to 350°F (180°C).
6. In the bowl of a stand mixer fitted with the paddle attachment, beat butter and granulated sugar at medium speed until light and creamy, 2 to 3 minutes, stopping to scrape sides of bowl. Add eggs, one at a time, beating well after each addition and stopping to scrape sides of bowl. Beat in vanilla, salt, and almond extract. With mixer on low speed, gradually add almond flour and all-purpose flour, beating until combined. Spoon mixture into a pastry bag, and cut a ¼-inch opening in tip.
7. Spread preserves in an even layer in bottom of prepared crust. Pipe almond flour mixture onto preserves; gently spread smooth with an offset spatula. Top with almonds.
8. Bake until center is set and top is golden brown, about 30 minutes. Let cool in pan for 20 minutes. Remove from pan, and let cool completely on a wire rack.
9. In a small bowl, whisk together confectioners' sugar and milk; drizzle or pipe onto tart as desired. Serve immediately, or let stand until glaze is set. Refrigerate in an airtight container for up to 3 days.

Poached Pear Buttermilk Tart

Makes 1 (9½-inch) tart

This stunning tart combines a tangy buttermilk filling with a wine-poached pear topping. Both the spiced pastry dough and poached pears can be made a day ahead.

---

1 (750-ml) bottle fruity white wine, such as Pinot Grigio
2½ cups (500 grams) granulated sugar, divided
2 cups (480 grams) water
3 tablespoons (45 grams) fresh lemon juice
2 cinnamon sticks
6 whole cloves
2 medium firm ripe Bartlett pears (404 grams), peeled, halved, stemmed, and cored
Ginger Pastry Crust Dough (recipe follows)
2 tablespoons (16 grams) all-purpose flour, plus more for dusting
¼ teaspoon kosher salt
⅔ cup (160 grams) whole buttermilk, room temperature
⅓ cup (80 grams) heavy whipping cream, room temperature
¼ cup (57 grams) unsalted butter, melted and cooled
1 large egg (50 grams), room temperature
1 large egg yolk (19 grams), room temperature
2 teaspoons (12 grams) vanilla bean paste
Garnish: finely chopped pistachios, sliced almonds, confectioners' sugar

1. In a large saucepan, bring wine, 2 cups (400 grams) granulated sugar, 2 cups (480 grams) water, lemon juice, cinnamon sticks, and cloves to a boil over medium-high heat, stirring occasionally until sugar dissolves. Reduce heat, and simmer for 5 minutes.
2. Add pears to wine mixture; place a piece of parchment paper on surface of wine mixture, pressing down slightly to help keep pears submerged. Cook, turning pears occasionally, until pears are fork-tender, 25 to 40 minutes. Using a slotted spoon, transfer pears to a medium heatproof bowl.
3. Discard cinnamon sticks and cloves. Increase heat to medium-high; cook wine mixture until reduced to 3 cups, 15 to 18 minutes. Remove from heat; pour wine mixture onto pears in bowl. Cover with plastic wrap, pressing wrap directly onto surface to keep pears submerged. Refrigerate for at least 1 hour or up to overnight.
4. Let pear wine mixture stand at room temperature until ready to use. Let Ginger Pastry Crust Dough stand at room temperature for 10 minutes. Spray a 9½-inch round fluted removable-bottom tart pan with baking spray with flour.
5. On a lightly floured surface, roll dough into a 12-inch circle (about ⅛ inch thick). Transfer dough to prepared pan, pressing into bottom and up sides; fold any overhanging dough inside, and press to create a double thickness. (It's OK if dough tears in spots; just press back together.) Using a small sharp knife, trim dough flush with sides of tart pan. Pinch sides lightly so dough sits about ⅛ inch above top edge of pan; use any extra dough to patch thinner spots in crust. Cover and freeze for 15 minutes.
6. Preheat oven to 350°F (180°C). Place tart pan on a parchment paper-lined rimmed baking sheet. Top frozen dough with a sheet of parchment paper, letting ends extend over edges of tart pan. Add pie weights.
7. Bake until edges are lightly browned, 15 to 20 minutes, rotating pan halfway through baking. Carefully remove parchment and weights. Bake until crust is dry and set, about 5 minutes more. Let cool on parchment-lined pan on a wire rack. Leave oven on.
8. In the bowl of a stand mixer fitted with the whisk attachment, beat flour, salt, and remaining ½ cup (100 grams) granulated sugar at low speed until combined. Add buttermilk, cream, melted butter, egg, egg yolk, and vanilla bean paste; beat at medium speed until smooth and well combined, stopping to scrape bottom and sides of bowl.
9. Using a slotted spoon, remove pear halves from wine mixture. Pat pears dry, and slice each half lengthwise into 8 wedges. Arrange wedges in a tight overlapping circular pattern along edge of prepared crust. Pour buttermilk mixture in center of crust, slightly tilting pan gently to evenly distribute between pears. (Pan will be full but will not overflow during baking.)
10. Bake until filling jiggles slightly in center when pan is gently shaken and an instant-read thermometer inserted in center registers 170°F (76°C) to 175°F

(79°C), 25 to 28 minutes. Let cool completely in pan on a wire rack. Just before serving, remove tart from pan, and garnish with pistachios, almonds, and confectioners' sugar, if desired. Refrigerate in an airtight container for up to 3 days.

Ginger Pastry Crust Dough

Makes 1 (9½-inch) crust

1¾ cups (219 grams) all-purpose flour
⅓ cup (67 grams) granulated sugar
1½ teaspoons (3 grams) ground ginger
½ teaspoon (1.5 grams) kosher salt
½ cup (113 grams) cold unsalted butter, cubed
1 large egg (50 grams), lightly beaten

1. In the work bowl of a food processor, pulse flour, sugar, ginger, and salt until combined. Add cold butter, and pulse until mixture resembles coarse crumbs. Add egg, and pulse just until dough comes together, stopping to scrape sides of bowl. (Mixture should be moist but not sticky and should hold together when pinched.)
2. Turn out dough, and shape into a disk. Wrap in plastic wrap, and refrigerate for at least 1 hour or up to overnight.

Fruit Tartlets

Makes 12 tarts

Using an inverted muffin pan to bake the tartlet dough on the outside of the muffin cups gives the shells a well-defined shape and crisp, flaky texture. Top your tartlets with any berry or fruit you like.

All-purpose flour, for dusting
Tartlet Dough (recipe follows)
Pastry Cream (recipe follows)
4 cups (about 560 grams) assorted fresh berries
½ cup (160 grams) apricot preserves
1 tablespoon (15 grams) water

1. Preheat oven to 350°F (180°C). Invert a 12-cup muffin pan.
2. On a lightly floured surface, roll Tartlet Dough to ⅛-inch thickness. Using a 3¾- to 4-inch round fluted cutter, cut 12 circles (about 16 grams each), rerolling scraps as necessary. Drape 1 circle onto bottom of each muffin cup. Prick each several times with a fork.
3. Bake until crusts are golden brown, 15 to 18 minutes. Let cool on pan for 10 minutes. Remove from pan, and let cool completely on a wire rack.
4. Whisk cold Pastry Cream until smooth; spoon or pipe about ¼ cup (85 grams) Pastry Cream into each tart shell. Top with berries.
5. In a small microwave-safe bowl, heat preserves and 1 tablespoon (15 grams) water just until warm; stir until combined. Strain mixture through a fine-mesh sieve, discarding solids. Gently brush preserves mixture onto fruit. Serve immediately.

Tartlet Dough

Makes 12 tartlet crusts

½ cup (113 grams) cold unsalted butter, cubed
1⅓ cups (167 grams) all-purpose flour
1 tablespoon (12 grams) granulated sugar
1 teaspoon (3 grams) kosher salt
1½ tablespoons (22.5 grams) whole milk
1 large egg yolk (19 grams)

1. Freeze butter until firm, about 10 minutes.
2. In the bowl of a stand mixer fitted with the paddle attachment, whisk together flour, sugar, and salt by hand. Add frozen butter, and beat at low speed until butter is broken into small pieces, about 1½ minutes. (If any large pieces of butter remain, squeeze between fingers to break up.)
3. In a small bowl, whisk together milk and egg yolk. With mixer on low speed, add milk mixture to flour mixture, beating just until moist clumps form. Transfer mixture to a large piece of plastic wrap. Using your hands, bring mixture together to form a cohesive dough. (It's fine if there are visible pieces of butter; that helps create a flaky crust.) Shape dough into a disk, and wrap in plastic wrap. Refrigerate for at least 1 hour or overnight. Let stand at room temperature for 10 to 15 minutes before rolling out.

Pastry Cream

Makes about 3 cups

3 cups (720 grams) whole milk
1 cup (200 grams) granulated sugar, divided
1 teaspoon (6 grams) vanilla bean paste
8 large egg yolks (149 grams)
¼ cup plus 3 tablespoons (56 grams) cornstarch
¼ teaspoon kosher salt
¼ cup (57 grams) unsalted butter, cubed and softened

1. In a large saucepan, heat milk, ½ cup (100 grams) sugar, and vanilla bean paste over medium heat, whisking frequently, until steaming. (Do not boil.)
2. In a large bowl, whisk together egg yolks, cornstarch, salt, and remaining ½ cup (100 grams) sugar. Gradually add warm milk mixture, whisking constantly. Pour egg mixture into saucepan; cook over medium heat, whisking constantly, until thickened and bubbly, 5 to 6 minutes.
3. Strain mixture through a fine-mesh sieve into a large bowl, discarding solids. Whisk in butter until melted and smooth. Cover with plastic wrap, pressing wrap directly onto surface of custard to prevent a skin from forming. Refrigerate until thick and cold before using, at least 4 hours or overnight.

Tarte au Citron

Makes 1 (9-inch) deep-dish tart

Rosemary adds a subtle savory note to the sweetness of this tart dough while the punch of lemon accents the mellow flavor of toasted pine nuts.

Pine Nut Dough (recipe follows)
1¾ cups (350 grams) granulated sugar
½ cup plus 1 tablespoon (71 grams) all-purpose flour
2 tablespoons (16 grams) cornstarch
½ teaspoon (1.5 grams) kosher salt
6 large eggs (300 grams)
6 large egg yolks (112 grams)
1 teaspoon (4 grams) vanilla extract
1½ cups (360 grams) fresh lemon juice
Garnish: Candied Lemon Slices (recipe follows)

1. Preheat oven to 325°F (170°C).
2. Press Pine Nut Dough into bottom and up sides of a 9-inch deep-dish round removable-bottom tart pan. Top with a piece of parchment paper, letting ends extend over edges of pan. Add pie weights.
3. Bake until lightly browned, about 15 minutes. Let cool slightly. Carefully remove parchment and weights.
4. Bake until golden brown and firm, about 10 minutes more. Remove from oven, and let cool slightly. Reduce oven temperature to 300°F (150°C).
5. In a medium bowl, whisk together sugar, flour, cornstarch, and salt. In large medium bowl, whisk together eggs, egg yolks, and vanilla. Whisk sugar mixture into egg mixture just until combined. Whisk in lemon juice until smooth. Pour filling into warm prepared crust.
6. Bake until edges are set but center jiggles slightly when pan is gently shaken, 30 to 40 minutes. Let cool completely on a wire rack. Refrigerate until cold before serving, at least 4 hours or overnight. Garnish with Candied Lemon Slices just before serving, if desired. Cover and refrigerate for up to 3 days.

Pine Nut Dough

Makes 1 (9-inch) deep-dish crust

1 cup (96 grams) finely ground toasted pine nuts
3 tablespoons (36 grams) granulated sugar
2 teaspoons (1 gram) chopped fresh rosemary
½ teaspoon (1.5 grams) kosher salt
1½ cups (188 grams) all-purpose flour
½ cup (113 grams) unsalted butter, softened
1 large egg yolk (19 grams)

1. In the work bowl of a food processor, pulse pine nuts, sugar, rosemary, and salt until combined. Add flour; pulse until finely ground.
2. In the bowl of a stand mixer fitted with the paddle attachment, beat nut mixture, butter, and egg yolk at medium speed until combined. Wrap dough in plastic wrap, and refrigerate for at least 10 minutes before using.

Candied Lemon Slices

Makes about 18 slices

3 lemons (370 grams)
1 cup (200 grams) granulated sugar
1 cup (240 grams) water

1. Using a mandoline, carefully slice lemons into paper-thin rounds; discard seeds.
2. In a medium bowl, gently stir together lemon slices and sugar. Let stand until sugar dissolves, about 30 minutes.
3. In a medium saucepan, bring lemon-sugar mixture and 1 cup (240 grams) water to a boil over high heat. Reduce heat to medium-low; simmer, stirring occasionally, until translucent, about 30 minutes, being careful not to let mixture caramelize.
4. Remove from heat, and let cool slightly. Strain mixture, reserving lemon slices. Place lemon slices on parchment paper; let dry at room temperature. (Lemons will be sticky.) Cover and freeze for up to 1 week.

Chocolate Cherry Tart

Makes 1 (9-inch) tart

My favorite ice cream, Ben & Jerry's Cherry Garcia, inspired this tart that's comprised of fluted chocolate crust, vanilla seed-speckled cream, plump red cherries, and rich chocolate curls. It'll have you swooning even on the most sweltering of days.

All-purpose flour, for dusting
Chocolate Tart Crust Dough (recipe follows)
3 ounces (85 grams) semisweet chocolate, finely chopped
1 tablespoon (14 grams) unsalted butter
¼ cup (60 grams) heavy whipping cream
Cherry Crème Légère (recipe follows)
¾ pound (340 grams) dark sweet cherries, pitted and halved (about 2½ cups)
Garnish: chocolate curls

1. On a lightly floured surface, roll Chocolate Tart Crust Dough to ⅛-inch thickness. Carefully transfer to a 9-inch round fluted removable-bottom tart pan, pressing dough into bottom and up sides. Using a small knife, trim excess dough. Prick bottom of dough all over with a fork. Refrigerate until firm, about 30 minutes.
2. Preheat oven to 325°F (160°C).
3. Top dough with a piece of parchment paper, letting ends extend over edges of pan. Add pie weights.
4. Bake until edges are set, about 15 minutes. Carefully remove parchment and weights. Bake until center is set and surface is dry, 5 to 7 minutes more. Let cool completely in pan on a wire rack.
5. In a medium microwave-safe bowl, place chopped chocolate and butter.
6. In a small microwave-safe bowl, heat cream on high in 15-second intervals just until it begins to steam (30 to 45 seconds total). Pour onto chocolate mixture; cover and let stand for 5 minutes. Whisk until melted and smooth. (If chocolate lumps remain, microwave for 10 seconds, and whisk again.) Spread chocolate mixture into cooled crust. Refrigerate until set, about 1 hour.
7. Spread Cherry Crème Légère onto cold ganache; arrange cherries on top. Refrigerate for 1 hour before serving. Garnish with chocolate curls just before serving, if desired. Refrigerate in an airtight container for up to 3 days.

Chocolate Tart Crust Dough

Makes 1 (9-inch) crust

1½ cups (188 grams) all-purpose flour
¾ cup (90 grams) confectioners' sugar
⅓ cup (25 grams) Dutch process cocoa powder
¼ teaspoon kosher salt
½ cup (113 grams) cold unsalted butter, cubed
1 large egg (50 grams)
1 large egg yolk (19 grams)

1. In the bowl of a stand mixer fitted with the paddle attachment, whisk together flour, confectioners' sugar, cocoa, and salt by hand. Add cold butter; beat at low speed until mixture resembles coarse meal. Add egg and egg yolk; beat until combined and a dough forms.
2. Turn out dough, and shape into a disk. Wrap in plastic wrap, and refrigerate until firm, about 2 hours. Let stand at room temperature for 10 to 15 minutes before rolling out.

Cherry Crème Légère

Makes 2½ cups

1 large egg (50 grams), room temperature
1 large egg yolk (19 grams), room temperature
3 tablespoons (36 grams) granulated sugar
3 tablespoons (24 grams) cornstarch
½ teaspoon (1.5 grams) kosher salt
1 cup (240 grams) whole milk
2 teaspoons (12 grams) vanilla bean paste
1½ teaspoons (7.5 grams) maraschino cherry juice or cherry liqueur
2 tablespoons (28 grams) unsalted butter, room temperature
¾ cup (180 grams) cold heavy whipping cream

1. In a medium bowl, whisk together egg, egg yolk, sugar, cornstarch, and salt.
2. In a small saucepan, heat milk, vanilla bean paste, and cherry juice or liqueur over medium heat, stirring frequently, just until steaming. (Do not boil.) Slowly add half of hot milk mixture to egg mixture, whisking constantly. Whisk egg mixture into remaining milk mixture in saucepan; bring to a boil over medium heat, whisking constantly. Cook, whisking constantly, until mixture is thickened, 2 to 3 minutes.
3. Strain custard through a fine-mesh sieve into a medium bowl, discarding solids. Whisk in butter until melted and smooth. Cover with plastic wrap, pressing wrap directly onto surface of custard to prevent a skin from forming. Refrigerate until thick and cold, at least 2 hours.
4. In the bowl of a stand mixer fitted with the whisk attachment, beat cold cream at medium-high speed until stiff peaks form, 2 to 3 minutes.
5. Whisk cold custard; stir one-fourth of whipped cream into custard. Gently fold remaining whipped cream into custard until combined. Use immediately.

Spiced Plum Linzer Torte

Makes 1 (10-inch) tart

Named after the city of Linz, Austria, the Linzer torte is a classic European pastry most commonly served during Christmastime. Traditionally made with a shortcrust dough accented with ground nuts, the Linzer torte displays a jewel-toned jam filling beneath a lattice crust.

- 1¾ cups (219 grams) all-purpose flour, plus more for dusting
- 1¼ cups (120 grams) finely ground hazelnut flour
- 1 cup (96 grams) superfine blanched almond flour
- ⅓ cup (67 grams) granulated sugar
- ⅓ cup (73 grams) firmly packed light brown sugar
- 1 tablespoon (3 grams) tightly packed orange zest
- ¾ teaspoon (2.25 grams) kosher salt
- ¾ teaspoon (1.5 grams) ground cinnamon
- ½ teaspoon (2.5 grams) baking powder
- ¼ teaspoon ground ginger
- ⅛ teaspoon ground nutmeg
- ⅛ teaspoon ground cloves
- ¾ cup plus 2 tablespoons (198 grams) cold unsalted butter, cubed
- 1 large egg (50 grams)
- 1 teaspoon (4 grams) vanilla extract
- 2 cups (600 grams) damson plum preserves
- Confectioners' sugar, for dusting

1. In the bowl of a stand mixer, whisk together flours, granulated sugar, brown sugar, orange zest, salt, cinnamon, baking powder, ginger, nutmeg, and cloves by hand until combined. Add cold butter; using the paddle attachment, beat at medium speed until mixture resembles coarse crumbs, 2 to 3 minutes. Add egg and vanilla; beat at low speed just until dough comes together, stopping to scrape bottom and sides of bowl and paddle. (Mixture should be moist but not sticky and should hold together when pinched.)

2. Turn out dough onto a work surface; reserve one-third of dough (about 278 grams), and cover with plastic wrap.

3. Spray sides of a 10-inch round fluted removable-bottom tart pan with baking spray with flour. Press remaining dough into bottom and up sides of prepared pan, trimming any excess with a small sharp knife; add any dough trimmings to reserved one-third of dough. Cover with plastic wrap.

4. Lightly dust a sheet of wax paper with all-purpose flour; place reserved dough on paper, and lightly dust top of dough with flour. Place another sheet of wax paper on dough, and roll dough into a 12-inch circle (about ⅛ inch thick); place on a baking sheet. Refrigerate rolled dough and dough in tart pan for 1 hour.

5. Preheat oven to 350°F (180°C).

6. Spread preserves into prepared crust.

7. Remove top wax paper from rolled dough; using a pastry cutter or pastry wheel, cut dough into 1-inch-wide strips. Gently arrange strips about ½ inch apart in a crisscross pattern on preserves; press strips into edges of dough in pan, trimming off excess to create a clean edge. (If dough becomes too soft to work with, refrigerate in 15-minute intervals as needed; a lightly floured large offset spatula can help move strips.) If additional dough strips are needed, reroll excess dough between lightly floured sheets of wax paper to ⅛-inch thickness. Refrigerate assembled tart for 20 minutes.

8. Bake until crust is golden brown and set and filling is starting to bubble, 30 to 35 minutes. Let cool completely in pan on a wire rack. Remove from pan, and dust with confectioners' sugar just before serving. Store in an airtight container for up to 3 days.

Making the Dough

In the bowl of a stand mixer, whisk together flours, granulated sugar, brown sugar, orange zest, salt, cinnamon, baking powder, ginger, nutmeg, and cloves by hand until combined. Add cold butter; using the paddle attachment, beat at medium speed until mixture resembles coarse crumbs, 2 to 3 minutes. Add egg and vanilla; beat at low speed just until dough comes together, stopping to scrape sides of bowl. (Mixture should be moist but not sticky and should hold together when pinched.) Turn out dough onto a work surface; reserve one-third of dough (about 278 grams), and cover with plastic wrap.

TIP: A stand mixer is the most efficient and foolproof method when making this dough. Unlike a food processor, a stand mixer gives you more control as you see the dough coming together.

Spray sides of a 10-inch round fluted removable-bottom tart pan with baking spray with flour. Press remaining dough into bottom and up sides of prepared pan; trim any excess with a small sharp knife, and add to reserved one-third of dough. Cover with plastic wrap.

TIP: After pressing the dough in the pan with your hands, press the bottom of a metal measuring cup into the pan to prevent the dough from sticking to your fingers while getting a nice, even layer of dough so it bakes evenly.

Creating the Top Crust

Lightly dust a sheet of wax paper with all-purpose flour; place reserved dough on prepared wax paper, and lightly dust top of dough with all-purpose flour. Place another sheet of wax paper on dough, and roll dough into a 12-inch circle (about ⅛ inch thick); place on a baking sheet.

TIP: One trick to rolling out a soft dough like this is to sandwich it between two sheets of wax paper to keep it from sticking as you work with it. You can use parchment paper in a pinch, but wax paper is thinner and slightly easier to handle for this recipe. The dough will stick to the paper just enough to keep it from sliding around from the pressure of the rolling pin, allowing you to roll out the dough effortlessly.

Remove top sheet of wax paper from rolled dough; using a pastry cutter or pastry wheel, cut dough into 1-inch-wide strips; cover and freeze until firm, about 15 minutes. Refrigerate rolled dough and dough in pan for 1 hour.

TIP: Use a ruler to score the rolled-out dough into 1-inch intervals. This serves as a guide to follow as you cut the entire length of the lattice strips using the help of the ruler's straight edge.

Spread preserves into prepared crust. Gently arrange strips about ½ inch apart in a crisscross pattern on preserves; press strips into edges of dough in pan, trimming off excess to create a clean edge. (If dough becomes too soft to work with, refrigerate in 15-minute intervals as needed; a lightly floured offset spatula can help move strips.) If additional dough strips are needed, reroll excess dough between lightly floured sheets of wax paper to ⅛-inch thickness. Refrigerate assembled tart for 20 minutes.

TIP: Refrigerating the assembled torte lets the butter in the dough solidify, which helps the crust bake up nice and crisp.

pâte viennoise

yeasted laminated and sweetened leavened dough

CROISSANTS, DANISH, BRIOCHE

When puff pastry and dairy-rich doughs are combined with yeast, the resulting array of baked goods is likely what first comes to mind when people think broadly of pastry. Though a case could be made that these are breads, their origin and distinct difference from baguettes and other basic French breads puts them in a category of their own.

Pâte Viennoise:
YEASTED LAMINATED AND SWEETENED LEAVENED DOUGH

Traditional Croissants

Makes 8 croissants

Croissants need no introduction. This pastry powerhouse is ubiquitous in bakeries and pâtisseries and the pinnacle challenge for the home baker. With patience, persistence, and the finest-quality European-style butter, this recipe and guide will help you reach laminated nirvana.

4½ cups (572 grams) bread flour
6 tablespoons (72 grams) granulated sugar
1 tablespoon (9 grams) plus ¼ teaspoon kosher salt, divided
2¼ teaspoons (7 grams) active dry yeast
1 cup (240 grams) warm whole milk (100°F/38°C to 110°F/43°C)
⅓ cup (80 grams) warm water (100°F/38°C to 110°F/43°C)
6 tablespoons (84 grams) unsalted European-style butter, room temperature
Butter Block (recipe follows)
1 large egg (50 grams)

1. In the bowl of a stand mixer fitted with the paddle attachment, beat flour, sugar, 1 tablespoon (9 grams) salt, and yeast at low speed just until combined.
2. In a small bowl, combine warm milk and ⅓ cup (80 grams) warm water. With mixer on low speed, add milk mixture to flour mixture in a slow, steady stream; beat for about 1 minute. Add butter, 2 tablespoons (28 grams) at a time, beating until combined after each addition; beat for 4 minutes. Increase mixer speed to medium-low, and beat until dough passes the windowpane test, about 3 minutes. (See Note.) (If your mixer seems to be having a hard time toward the end, finish kneading by hand.)
3. Divide dough in half; shape each half into a ball. Place each dough ball on a parchment paper-lined baking sheet, and wrap in plastic wrap. Refrigerate overnight, or let stand at room temperature for 30 minutes and then refrigerate for 3½ hours.
4. Punch down each dough ball. Cover 1 dough ball. Roll uncovered dough ball into a 12x8-inch rectangle; repeat with remaining dough. Quickly place Butter Block directly on top of 1 dough rectangle. Cover with remaining dough rectangle, creating a "butter sandwich." Pinch together edges of top and bottom doughs to seal. Working quickly and carefully, roll into a 24x9-inch rectangle. (Be careful not to tear dough or allow any butter to leak out.) Trim about ½ inch off short sides so butter layer is exposed. Fold dough in half so short sides meet; lightly press dough at fold to mark center. Unfold dough. Fold short sides of dough to meet in center. Fold one half of dough onto other half of dough as if you are closing a book. (This is called a book-fold; at this point, you should have 4 layers of dough.) Return dough to pan, and wrap in plastic wrap. Freeze for 15 minutes; refrigerate for 20 minutes.
5. Roll dough into a 30x9-inch rectangle. Trim about ¼ to ½ inch off short sides so butter layers are exposed. Fold dough in half so short sides meet. Pat fold to mark center. Unfold dough, and pull one short side to center. Pull opposite side to center so short ends are touching. Pinch seams together; fold along center seam, like closing a book. (Your dough will be thinner this time.) Return to pan, and wrap in plastic wrap. Freeze for 15 minutes; refrigerate for 20 minutes.
6. Line 2 baking sheets with parchment paper.
7. Bring a small saucepan of water to a boil over medium-high heat. Place pan of just-boiled water in back right corner of cold oven. Keep oven door closed. (This gets your oven steamy but also allows the space to cool a bit while you're shaping the dough.)
8. Roll dough into an 18x12-inch rectangle. Trim short sides so butter layers are exposed. Trim ¼ inch off long sides. Cover dough, and freeze for 8 to 10 minutes.
9. Working quickly, cut dough into 4 (12x4-inch) rectangles. Cut each rectangle diagonally to create 8 triangles. Make a 1-inch cut from center of 4-inch base of each triangle. Very gently stretch triangle to relax dough. Fold center corners of base toward sharpest point of triangle, and roll dough into a log toward sharpest point. Place, point side down, about 3½ inches apart on prepared pans. Let rise in prepared oven for 2½ hours. (Try not to place pans directly over steamy water. Do not open oven door while proofing. Croissants will double in size, have a little separation in their layers, and be light as a feather.)
10. Remove croissants and saucepan of water from oven. Loosely cover croissants with greased plastic wrap. (Do not secure plastic wrap. You don't want to put any weight or pressure on proofed dough.) Refrigerate until oven is preheated.

11. Position oven racks in center and top of oven. Preheat oven to 425°F (220°C).
12. In a small bowl, whisk together egg and remaining ¼ teaspoon salt. Brush croissants with egg wash.
13. Bake on center rack for 5 minutes. Place a sheet of foil on top rack, and reduce oven temperature to 375°F (190°C). Bake for 5 minutes more. Rotate pans, and bake for 8 to 10 minutes more.

Note: *To use the windowpane test to check dough for proper gluten development, lightly flour hands and pinch off (don't tear) a small piece of dough. Slowly pull the dough out from the center. If the dough is ready, you will be able to stretch it until it's thin and translucent like a windowpane. If the dough tears, it's not quite ready. Beat for 1 minute, and test again.*

Butter Block

Makes 1 (11x7-inch) rectangle

1 **cup (227 grams) cold unsalted European-style butter**

1. Cut butter into 4 rectangles.
2. Fold a 24x8-inch sheet of parchment paper in half to create a 12x8-inch rectangle. Unfold parchment, and place butter on one side. Pull other half of parchment over butter. Using a rolling pin, pound butter into an 11x7-inch rectangle. (Try not to roll butter, as it creates friction and heat. You want it to stay as cold as possible.) Freeze for 5 minutes; refrigerate until ready to use. (This can be made a day ahead.)

Traditional Croissants: Make the Butter Block

All luscious lamination begins with a golden building block, a.k.a. the butter block. Here's how to start off your lamination journey on the right foot.

Cut butter into 4 rectangles. Fold a 24x8-inch sheet of parchment paper in half to create a 12x8-inch rectangle. Unfold parchment, and place butter on one side.

TIP: You want to work with cold butter but not frozen butter. If the butter is too soft, it'll ooze out during shaping; too hard and you'll wear out your arm.

Using a rolling pin, pound butter into an 11x7-inch rectangle. (Try not to roll butter, as it creates friction and heat. You want it to stay as cold as possible.)

TIP: As you near the finish line for hammering out the butter, one roll to smooth things out won't hurt—just make sure that you're doing it as a final touch to make things level.

Freeze for 5 minutes; refrigerate until ready to use. (This can be made a day ahead.)

TIP: If at any point your butter becomes too soft at the edges and goes outside of its rectangular boundaries, use an offset spatula or bench scraper to smooth and coax the errant butter back into line.

Traditional Croissants: Knead to Know

Croissant dough can be kneaded in a mixer, but sometimes the best way to know when your dough is ready is to get a little hands-on. Give your mixer a rest and finish it by hand.

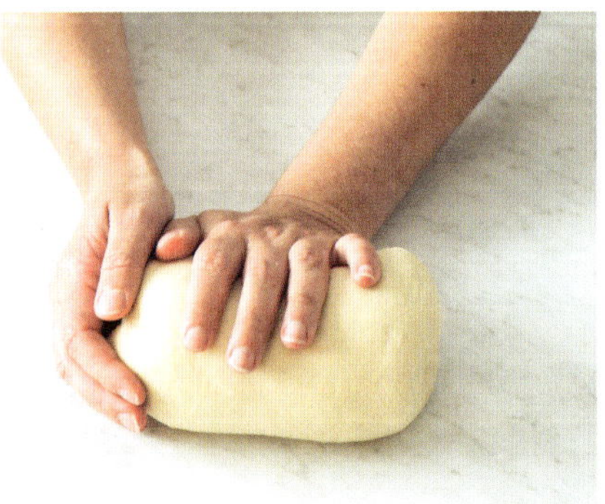

Turn out dough onto a lightly floured surface.

TIP: Be scant with the flour, as you don't want excess gluten to ruin your lamination work down the road. Also, while the recipe calls for bread flour, make sure you're using softer -protein all-purpose flour for dusting your hands and surface.

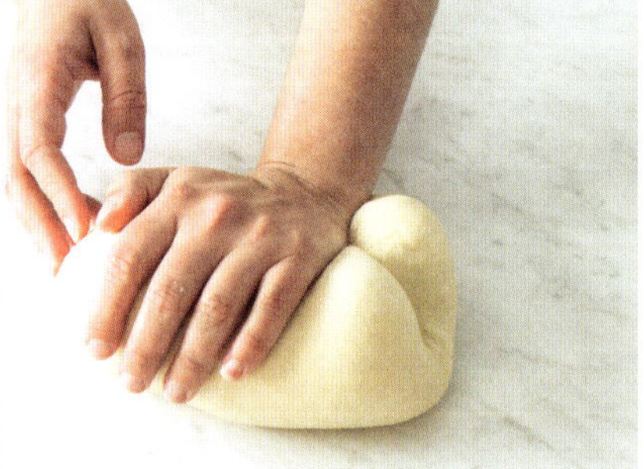

Fold dough in half toward you; using heels of your hands, push dough away.

TIP: This is the basic hand movement for all kneading and can be used on many bread doughs. Perform this for a couple of minutes and then conduct the windowpane test to confirm proper gluten development.

Divide dough in half. (Use a scale for accuracy.) Lightly cup and roll each half to form a rough ball.

TIP: This a gentle shaping, so try not to get too rough with your dough.

Traditional Croissants Timeline

Pick one of these two timelines to make the Traditional Croissants either a one-day or a weekend project

1-day timeline

8–8:45 a.m. Make croissant dough and shape into rounds. Let stand at room temperature for 30 minutes. As dough rests, make Butter Block, and refrigerate until ready to use.
8:45 a.m. Refrigerate dough for 3½ hours.
12:15–12:45 p.m. Remove dough and Butter Block from refrigerator. Shape dough into rectangles. Sandwich Butter Block between two rectangles and roll into a 24x9-inch rectangle. Perform first book-fold.
12:45 p.m. Freeze dough for 15 minutes. Refrigerate for 20 minutes.
1:20–1:55 p.m. Perform second book-fold. Freeze dough for 15 minutes. Refrigerate for 20 minutes. While dough is chilling, prep oven for proofing.
2:30–2:50 p.m. Shape croissants.
2:50 p.m. Proof shaped croissants in prepared oven for 2½ hours.
5:20 p.m. Remove proofed croissants from oven; cover and refrigerate. Preheat oven.
5:40 p.m. Brush with egg wash, and bake as directed.

3-day timeline

Day 1

5 p.m. Make Butter Block; refrigerate overnight.
5:30 p.m. Make dough; refrigerate overnight.

Day 2

10–10:30 a.m. Remove dough and Butter Block from refrigerator. Shape dough into rectangles. Sandwich Butter Block between two rectangles and roll into a 24x9-inch rectangle. Perform first book-fold.
10:30 a.m. Freeze dough for 15 minutes. Refrigerate for 20 minutes.
11:05–11:35 a.m. Perform second book-fold. Freeze dough for 15 minutes. Refrigerate for 20 minutes.
12:10 p.m. Shape croissants. Cover and refrigerate overnight.

Day 3

7 a.m. Prep oven for proofing. Let shaped croissants proof in oven for 2½ to 3 hours.
10 a.m. Remove proofed croissants from oven; cover and refrigerate. Preheat oven.
10:20 a.m. Brush with egg wash, and bake as directed.

Pâte Viennoise:
YEASTED LAMINATED AND SWEETENED LEAVENED DOUGH

Genius Quick Croissants

Makes 8 croissants

Introducing my new and improved way to roll! Made with the same ingredients as the traditional but with a less-fussy, beginner-friendly method, these croissants are the gateway baked good to the world of lamination.

⅓ cup (80 grams) water
6 tablespoons (72 grams) granulated sugar, divided
2¼ teaspoons (7 grams) active dry yeast
4½ cups (572 grams) bread flour
3¾ teaspoons (10.5 grams) kosher salt, divided
1 cup (227 grams) plus 6 tablespoons (84 grams) cold unsalted European-style butter, cut into ¾-inch cubes
1 cup (240 grams) cold whole milk
All-purpose flour, for dusting
1 large egg (50 grams)

1. In a small microwave-safe bowl, stir together ⅓ cup (80 grams) water and ½ teaspoon (2 grams) sugar; heat on high in 10-second intervals until an instant-read thermometer registers 110°F (43°C) to 115°F (46°C). Whisk in yeast until well combined. Let stand until foamy, 5 to 10 minutes.
2. In the bowl of a stand mixer fitted with the paddle attachment, beat bread flour, 3½ teaspoons (10.5 grams) salt, and remaining 5 tablespoons plus 2½ teaspoons (70 grams) sugar at low speed until combined. Add 6 tablespoons (84 grams) cold butter; pulse mixer between low speed and "off" setting until mixture resembles coarse bread crumbs, about 3 minutes. Add remaining 1 cup (227 grams) cold butter; pulse mixer between low speed and "off" setting just until butter is coated with flour.
3. Add cold milk to yeast mixture; while pulsing mixer between low speed and "off" setting, add yeast mixture to flour mixture in a slow, steady stream just until a shaggy dough comes together. (There will still be large pieces of butter.)
4. Lightly dust work surface with all-purpose flour. Turn out dough onto prepared surface, and shape into a rough 7-inch square. (Dough will be soft and slightly sticky.) Wrap in plastic wrap, and freeze for 30 minutes.
5. Lightly dust work surface with all-purpose flour. On prepared surface, roll dough into an 18x9-inch rectangle, lightly dusting surface and top of dough with all-purpose flour as needed. Fold dough in half so short sides meet. Pat fold to mark center. Unfold dough, and pull one short side to center. Pull opposite side to center so short sides are touching. Pinch seams together; fold along center seam, like closing a book. Rotate dough 90 degrees; repeat rolling and folding procedure once. (Dough will start out soft, rough, and somewhat sticky but will come together; turn dough over as needed so edges are rolled out as evenly as possible.) Wrap in plastic wrap, and freeze for 15 minutes.
6. Repeat rotating, rolling, and folding process once. Wrap in plastic wrap, and freeze for 10 minutes. (If dough is resisting or feels too soft, wrap in plastic wrap and freeze for 10 to 15 minutes before continuing.) Wrap in plastic wrap, and refrigerate for 1½ hours.
7. Position oven racks in top third and bottom third of oven. Line 2 baking sheets with parchment paper.
8. Bring a small saucepan of water to a boil over medium-high heat. Place pan of just-boiled water in back right corner of cold oven. Keep oven door closed. (This gets your oven steamy but also allows the space to cool a bit while you're shaping the dough.)
9. Lightly dust work surface with all-purpose flour. On prepared surface, roll dough into an 18x12½-inch rectangle (about ¼ inch thick). (If dough or butter feels too soft, wrap in plastic wrap and freeze for 10 to 15 minutes before continuing.) Using a pastry cutter or pastry wheel, trim dough into a 16x12-inch rectangle; cut into 4 (12x4-inch) rectangles. Cut each rectangle diagonally to create 8 triangles. Make a 1-inch cut from center of 4-inch base of each triangle. Cover with plastic wrap, and freeze for 10 minutes.
10. Very gently stretch triangles to about 16 inches long. Starting at wide base of each triangle, fold center corners of 1-inch cut toward sharpest point of dough; roll dough into a log toward sharpest point. Place, point side down, 2½ to 3 inches apart on prepared pans. (Shape and proof dough scraps, if desired.) Let rise in prepared oven until croissants are very puffed and jiggle slightly when pan is wiggled, 2 to 3 hours. (Temperature

Genius Quick Croissants Timeline

These clever croissants can be tackled in seven hours or two days—you pick your pace

1-day timeline

8–8:15 a.m. Make dough. Freeze for 30 minutes.
8:45–9:05 a.m. Perform 2 book-folds.
9:05 a.m. Freeze for 15 minutes.
9:20–9:40 a.m. Perform third book-fold. Refrigerate dough for 1½ hours. During the last 20 minutes of chilling, prep oven for proofing.
11:10–11:30 a.m. Shape croissants.
11:30 a.m. Proof shaped croissants in prepared oven for 2 to 3 hours.
2:30 p.m. Remove proofed croissants from oven; cover and refrigerate. Preheat oven.
2:50 p.m. Brush with egg wash, and bake as directed.

2-day timeline

Day 1

10–10:15 a.m. Make dough. Freeze for 30 minutes.
10:45–11:05 a.m. Perform 2 book-folds.
11:05 a.m. Freeze for 15 minutes.
11:20–11:40 a.m. Perform third book-fold. Refrigerate dough for 1½ hours.
1:10 p.m. Shape croissants. Cover and refrigerate overnight.

Day 2

7 a.m. Prep oven for proofing. Let shaped croissants proof in oven for 2½ to 3 hours.
10 a.m. Remove proofed croissants from oven; cover and refrigerate. Preheat oven.
10:20 a.m. Brush croissants with egg wash. Bake as directed.

within oven should be 75°F/24°C to 79°F/26°C; higher temperatures may cause butter in croissants to melt.)

11. Remove croissants and saucepan of water from oven. Loosely cover croissants with greased plastic wrap. (Do not secure plastic wrap. You don't want to put any weight or pressure on proofed dough.) Refrigerate until oven is preheated.

12. Position oven rack in center of oven. Preheat oven to 425°F (220°C).

13. In a small bowl, whisk together egg and remaining ¼ teaspoon salt. Brush croissants with egg wash. (Avoid applying or leaving pools of egg wash.)

14. Bake, one pan at a time, for 10 minutes, loosely covering with foil after 6 minutes of baking. Rotate pan, and reduce oven temperature to 375°F (190°C); bake until golden brown and an instant-read thermometer inserted in center registers 210°F (98°C), 8 to 10 minutes more.

Genius Quick Croissants: Mixing Magic

Genius Quick Croissants begin in the stand mixer, incorporating the butter in two ways for one flawless recipe

In the bowl of a stand mixer fitted with the paddle attachment, beat bread flour, 3½ teaspoons (10.5 grams) salt, and remaining 5 tablespoons plus 2½ teaspoons (70 grams) sugar at low speed until combined. Add 6 tablespoons (84 grams) cold butter; pulse mixer between low speed and "off" setting until mixture resembles coarse bread crumbs, about 3 minutes.
TIP: Think of this first butter incorporation like you're pulling together a mealy pie dough. You want the butter to be mixed in well so only a close observer can see its coarsely sandy texture.

Add remaining 1 cup (227 grams) cold butter; pulse mixer between low speed and "off" setting just until butter is coated with flour.
TIP: Unlike the previous butter used, we don't want this addition to be smoothly incorporated. Essentially, you're treating your stand mixer like a food processor, working in pulses rather than in smooth increments. The added benefit of the stand mixer is its gentle touch, lightly coating the butter in flour when a food processor would pulverize.

Add cold milk to yeast mixture; while pulsing mixer between low speed and "off" setting, add yeast mixture to flour mixture in a slow, steady stream just until a shaggy dough comes together. (There will still be large pieces of butter.)
TIP: This is a crucial step, so stay vigilant. Your goal is to make a rough, shaggy dough, not to work in the butter chunks. Overmixing at this step will diminish your lamination.

Lightly dust work surface with all-purpose flour. Turn out dough, and shape into a rough 7-inch square.
TIP: As you can see, our dough is very loosely mixed, packed with butter chunks, and looking like particularly rich rough puff. The dough still requires some pressing and cajoling to become one unified dough.

Dough will be soft and slightly sticky.
TIP: Like with all other forms of lamination, try to work quickly. Don't fuss over making the perfect square—the softness and stickiness of the dough means it's ready for a cooldown.

Wrap in plastic wrap, and freeze for 30 minutes.
TIP: Unlike our Traditional Croissants dough, our Genius Quick Croissants dough relies on the extra chill of the freezer rather than the refrigerator. Our chunky butter is slightly more vulnerable to the heat and needs a helping hand.

Genius Quick Croissants: The Book Fold

The book-fold, also known as the four-fold, is what gives the dough layers. Each time you complete a book-fold, you're quadrupling your layers.

Lightly dust work surface with all-purpose flour. Roll dough into an 18x9-inch rectangle, lightly dusting surface and top of dough with all-purpose flour as needed.

TIP: Be scant with the flour, as you don't want excess gluten to ruin your texture.

Fold dough in half so short sides meet. Pat fold to mark center.

TIP: You can use either a light fold in half or a ruler to mark your rectangle's center. The main thing is to make a visual mark to know where you need to aim for your first fold.

Unfold dough, and pull one short side to center.

TIP: If you're a little nervous about conducting your first book-fold on your croissant dough, try practicing a few times on paper. It's much more forgiving and a lot less heat-sensitive.

Pull opposite side to center so short ends are touching.

TIP: If you've measured everything correctly and made that helpful center mark—you did, right?—the two ends should meet nicely together, no egregious overlap.

Pinch seams together.

TIP: Your dough is still fairly elastic and wants to spring back into shape. Pinching the seams together helps keep the dough ends from snapping away from each other.

Fold along center seam like closing a book. Rotate dough 90 degrees; repeat rolling and folding procedure once. Dough will start out soft, rough, and somewhat sticky but will come together; turn dough over as needed so edges are rolled out as evenly as possible.

TIP: What starts out rough will become nicely smooth with the second book-fold.

Classic Crescent

Here's where the two croissant methods, traditional and quick, meet again. Both doughs are shaped the same way.

Using a pastry cutter or pastry wheel, trim dough into a 16x12-inch rectangle; cut into 4 (12x4-inch) rectangles. Cut each rectangle diagonally to create 8 triangles. Make a small 1-inch cut from center of 4-inch base of each triangle. Wrap in plastic wrap, and freeze for 10 minutes. Very gently stretch triangles to about 16 inches long. Starting at 4-inch base of each triangle, fold center corners of 1-inch cut toward sharpest point of dough; roll dough into a log toward sharpest point. Place, point side down, 2½ to 3 inches apart on prepared pans (4 per pan).

Traditional and Quick

No matter which you choose, you'll be rewarded with layer upon layer of flaky, buttery goodness

No matter what croissant shape you choose, you'll have some leftover dough scraps. Don't toss these tasty trimmings! Instead, shape, proof, fill, and bake the scraps as desired.

Shaped croissants can be covered and refrigerated overnight or covered and frozen until solid. Proof and bake the next day as directed, increasing proofing or baking time as needed.

Pain au Chocolat

Makes 8 croissants

All-purpose flour, for dusting
Traditional Croissants (recipe on page 88) or Genius Quick Croissants (recipe on page 92)
16 chocolate batons (baking sticks)
Turbinado sugar, for sprinkling (optional)

1. Proceed with Traditional Croissants recipe or Genius Quick Croissants recipe through step 8.
2. On a lightly floured surface, roll dough into an 18x12½-inch rectangle (about ¼ inch thick). Using a pastry cutter or pastry wheel, trim dough rectangle into a 14x12-inch rectangle; cut into 4 (12x3½-inch) rectangles. Cut each rectangle crosswise to create 8 (6x3½-inch) rectangles. Cover with plastic wrap, and freeze for 10 minutes. Re-stretch dough rectangles to 6 inches in length, if needed.
3. Trim end of chocolate batons, if necessary. Place 1 baton along a short side of 1 dough rectangle. Roll up dough into a log once around baton. Place another chocolate baton where short side meets inside of dough; continue to roll until seam side down. Lightly pat top of dough to help secure. Using a sharp knife, score top of dough, if desired.
4. Proceed with Traditional Croissants or Genius Quick Croissants recipe as directed. Sprinkle turbinado sugar (if using) after egg wash.

Ham-and-Cheese Croissants

Makes 8 croissants

Traditional Croissants (recipe on page 88) or Genius Quick Croissants (recipe on page 92)
8 thin slices ham
3 thin slices Gruyère cheese, cut into 3x½-inch strips

1. Proceed with Traditional Croissants recipe or Genius Quick Croissants recipe through step 8.
2. On a lightly floured surface, roll dough into an 18x12½-inch rectangle (about ¼ inch thick). Using a pastry cutter or pastry wheel, trim dough rectangle into a 14x12-inch rectangle; cut into 4 (12x3½-inch) rectangles. Cut each rectangle crosswise to create 8 (6x3½-inch) rectangles. Cover with plastic wrap, and freeze for 10 minutes. Re-stretch dough rectangles to 6 inches in length, if needed.
3. Place 1 thin piece of ham on top of 1 dough rectangle so edge is flush with a short side of rectangle; top with 1 cheese piece Roll up dough into a log once completely around cheese and ham. Place another piece of cheese where short side meets ham and inside of dough; continue to roll until seam side down. Lightly pat top of dough to help secure. Using a sharp knife, score top of dough, if desired.
4. Proceed with Traditional Croissants or Genius Quick Croissants recipe as directed.

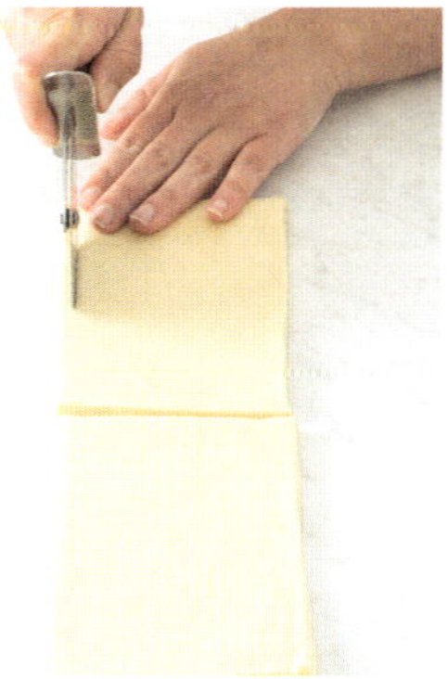

Filled Rectangle

Using a pastry cutter or pastry wheel, trim dough rectangle into a 14x12-inch rectangle; cut into 4 (12x3½-inch) rectangles. Slice each rectangle crosswise to create 8 (6x3½-inch) rectangles. Wrap in plastic wrap, and freeze for 10 minutes. Re-stretch dough rectangle to 6 inches in length, if needed. Trim chocolate batons to correct length, if necessary. Place 1 baton along one short side of 1 dough rectangle. Roll up dough into a log once completely around baton. Place another chocolate baton where short side meets inside of dough; continue to roll until seam side down. Lightly pat top of dough to help secure. Using a sharp razor or knife, score top of dough, if desired.

Croissant Loaf

Makes 1 (8½x4½-inch) loaf

All-purpose flour, for dusting
Traditional Croissants (recipe on page 88) or Genius Quick Croissants (recipe on page 92)

1. Proceed with Traditional Croissants recipe or Genius Quick Croissants recipe through step 8.
2. Spray an 8½x4½-inch loaf pan with cooking spray. Line pan with parchment paper, letting excess extend over sides of pan.
3. On a lightly floured surface, roll dough into an 18x12½-inch rectangle (about ¼ inch thick). Using a pastry cutter or pastry wheel, trim dough rectangle into a 12x10-inch rectangle. Working quickly, cut into 4 (10x3-inch) rectangles. Cover with plastic wrap, and freeze for 10 minutes.
4. In prepared pan, arrange dough in a zigzag ribbonlike pattern, leaving about a ½-inch border around edges. (Dough will not completely fill pan at this point but will grow as its proofs.) Proof as directed in Traditional Croissants or Genius Quick Croissants recipe. Loosely cover proofed loaf with greased plastic wrap, and refrigerate while oven preheats.
5. Position oven rack in center of oven. Preheat oven to 425°F (220°C).
6. Uncover loaf, egg wash, and place on center rack of oven.
7. Immediately reduce oven temperature to 375°F (190°C). Bake for 18 minutes; loosely cover with foil, and bake until golden brown and an instant-read thermometer inserted in center registers 210°F (98°C), 32 to 42 minutes more. Let cool in pan for 10 minutes. Using excess parchment as handles, remove from pan, and let cool completely on a wire rack. Store in an airtight container for up to 3 days.

Lovely Loaf

Using a pastry cutter or pastry wheel, trim dough rectangle into a 12x10-inch rectangle. Working quickly, cut into 4 (10x3-inch) rectangles. Cover with plastic wrap, and freeze for 10 minutes. In prepared pan, arrange dough in a zigzag ribbonlike pattern, leaving about a ½-inch border around edges. Dough will not completely fill pan at this point but will grow as its proofs.

Danish Dough

This Danish recipe is a great way to get started with yeasted laminated doughs. The most important thing to remember is that pastry can smell fear. Be confident! You are the boss! Now, go own this dough.

Dough:
1 cup (240 grams) warm whole milk (110°F/43°C)
2 tablespoons plus 2 teaspoons (24 grams) active dry yeast
4½ cups (563 grams) all-purpose flour, plus more for dusting
⅓ cup (70 grams) granulated sugar
¼ cup (67 grams) unsalted butter, softened
1 tablespoon (9 grams) kosher salt
1 tablespoon (6 grams) orange zest
3 large eggs (150 grams)

Butter block:
1¾ cups (397 grams) unsalted butter, softened
2 tablespoons (16 grams) all-purpose flour
1 teaspoon (3 grams) kosher salt

1. For dough: In a small bowl, combine warm milk and yeast. Let stand until foamy, 7 to 10 minutes.
2. In the bowl of a stand mixer fitted with the dough hook attachment, beat flour, sugar, butter, salt, and zest at low speed until combined, 2 to 3 minutes. Add yeast mixture and eggs, beating just until combined.
3. Turn out dough onto a lightly floured surface, and knead 2 to 3 times until a smooth ball forms. Wrap in plastic wrap, and refrigerate for at least 2 hours or overnight.
4. For butter block: In the bowl of a stand mixer fitted with the paddle attachment, beat butter, flour, and salt on medium until creamy and well combined, about 2 minutes, stopping to scrape sides of bowl. On a piece of plastic wrap, shape butter mixture into a 12x10-inch rectangle, keeping sides as straight as possible. Wrap in plastic wrap, and refrigerate for at least 30 minutes or overnight.
5. Let dough and butter block stand at room remperature until butter is pliable, about 10 minutes.
6. On a lightly floured surface, roll dough into an 18x10-inch rectangle. Unwrap butter block, and place it on bottom two-thirds of dough. Fold dough in thirds like a letter, and roll to 18x10-inch rectangle. Rotate dough 90 degrees; fold into thirds like a letter. Wrap dough in plastic wrap, and refrigerate for 1 hour.
7. Repeat rolling and folding procedure two more times, refrigerating for at least 1 hour between turns. After final rolling and folding, wrap dough in plastic wrap, and refrigerate for at least 8 hours or overnight.

pro tip

Danish Dough freezes well, so you can bake a few small batches of pastries when you want. Let it thaw completely in the refrigerator before using.

Cream Cheese-and-Jam Danish

Makes 12 Danish

Rich and smooth, fruity and tangy, this is the classic Danish that all bakers need in their repertoire. Use any jam you like.

Danish Dough (recipe on page 102)
All-purpose flour, for dusting
Cream Cheese Filling (recipe follows)
1 cup (320 grams) cherry jam
1 large egg (50 grams), beaten
1 cup (115 grams) sliced almonds
Garnish: confectioners' sugar

1. Line baking sheets with parchment paper.
2. Cut Danish Dough in half; refrigerate one portion. Lightly flour a work surface. On prepared surface, roll dough to a 12x8-inch rectangle. Using a pastry cutter or pastry wheel, cut dough into 6 (4-inch) squares. Fold corners of squares in center, and lightly press with your fingertip to adhere. Place 2 inches apart on prepared pans. Repeat procedure with remaining portion of dough. Loosely cover pans with plastic wrap, and let stand for 30 minutes.
3. Preheat oven to 375°F (190°C).
4. Spoon about 1 teaspoon (8 grams) Cream Cheese Filling onto center of each pastry. Top with about 1 teaspoon (7 grams) jam. Brush egg onto dough.
5. Bake until golden brown, 15 to 20 minutes. Sprinkle almonds onto hot Danish. Remove from pans, and let cool completely on wire racks. Garnish with confectioners' sugar, if desired. Store in an airtight container for up to 2 days.

Cream Cheese Filling

Makes about 1 cup

1 (8-ounce) package (226 grams) cream cheese, softened
1 cup (120 grams) confectioners' sugar
1 large egg yolk (19 grams)
1 teaspoon (6 grams) vanilla bean paste
½ teaspoon (1.5 grams) kosher salt

1. In the bowl of a stand mixer fitted with the paddle attachment, beat all ingredients at medium speed until smooth and creamy, 2 to 3 minutes, stopping to scrape bottom and sides of bowl and paddle.

Bacon, Egg, and Cheese Danish

Makes 12 Danish

Salty bacon and sharp pecorino pair perfectly
with a sunny-side up egg on these savory Danish.

All-purpose flour, for dusting
Danish Dough (recipe on page 102)
1 large egg (50 grams), lightly beaten
12 medium eggs (612 grams)
4 ounces (114 grams) pecorino cheese, finely shredded (about 1 cup)
2 teaspoons (3 grams) kosher salt
2 teaspoons (4 grams) ground black pepper
8 slices bacon, cooked and crumbled
Garnish: chopped fresh chives

1. Line baking sheets with parchment paper.
2. Cut Danish Dough in half; refrigerate one portion. Lightly flour a work surface. On prepared surface, roll dough to a 16x12-inch rectangle. Using a pastry cutter or pastry wheel, cut dough into 12 (4-inch) squares. Using a 2½-inch round cutter, cut circles from half of squares. Place 6 whole squares 2 inches apart on prepared pans, and brush with beaten egg. Place squares with cutouts on top. Repeat procedure with remaining portion of dough. Loosely cover pans with plastic wrap, and let stand for 30 minutes.
3. Preheat oven to 375°.
4. Brush squares with beaten egg.
5. Bake for 7 to 8 minutes. Remove from oven, and crack one egg into center of each Danish. Sprinkle with cheese, salt, and pepper. Return to oven, and bake until eggs are set and pastry is puffed and golden brown, 10 to 15 minutes more. Sprinkle with bacon; garnish with chives, if desired. Serve warm.

Cinnamon Sugar Morning Buns

Makes 14 to 18 buns

These are a callback to the cinnamon sugar-packed original morning bun but done one better with a generous sprinkle of crunchy, toasty pecans.

Danish Dough (recipe on page 102)
½ cup (113 grams) unsalted butter, melted and divided
⅓ cup (67 grams) granulated sugar, plus more for sprinkling
All-purpose flour, for dusting
½ cup (110 grams) firmly packed dark brown sugar
2 tablespoons (12 grams) ground cinnamon
½ teaspoon (1.5 grams) kosher salt
⅔ cup (75 grams) chopped pecans
Cinnamon sugar (see Note)

1. Freeze Danish Dough for 15 to 30 minutes.
2. Brush 14 to 18 muffin cups with 2 tablespoons (28 grams) melted butter. Sprinkle with granulated sugar, tapping out excess.
3. On a lightly floured surface, roll cold dough into an 18x12-inch rectangle.
4. In a small bowl, whisk together brown sugar, granulated sugar, cinnamon, and salt.
5. Using a pastry brush, brush remaining ¼ cup plus 2 tablespoons (85 grams) melted butter onto dough. Sprinkle brown sugar mixture onto butter, leaving a ½-inch border along one long edge; sprinkle with pecans. Starting at long side opposite border, roll up dough into a log. Trim edges if desired, and cut crosswise into 1-inch-thick slices.
6. Place slices, cut side up, in prepared muffin cups, gently pressing down until dough fills cups. Cover and let rise in a warm, draft-free place (75°F/24°C) until puffed, 45 minutes to 1 hour.
7. Preheat oven to 375°F (190°C).
8. Bake until golden brown and an instant-read thermometer inserted in center registers 210°F (99°C), 20 to 25 minutes, covering with foil halfway through baking to prevent excess browning if necessary. Let cool in pans for 10 minutes. Remove from pans, and dredge in cinnamon sugar. Serve warm.

Note: *For cinnamon sugar, in a small bowl, whisk together 1 cup (200 grams) granulated sugar and 1 tablespoon (6 grams) ground cinnamon.*

Meyer Lemon Morning Buns

Makes 14 to 18 buns

Inspired by the orange-infused morning buns available at Tartine in San Francisco, California, I decided to imbue this sunny version with my reigning star of winter citrus: Meyer lemon. After packing a hint of warm cardamom within its tight spiral, I like to finish off this tangy triumph with a bright blueberry sugar coating.

Danish Dough (recipe on page 102)
½ cup (113 grams) unsalted butter, melted and divided
Granulated sugar, for sprinkling
All-purpose flour, for dusting
Meyer lemon sugar (see Notes)
¼ teaspoon ground cardamom
Blueberry sugar (see Notes)

1. Freeze Danish Dough for 15 to 30 minutes.
2. Brush 14 to 18 muffin cups with 2 tablespoons (28 grams) melted butter. Sprinkle with granulated sugar, tapping out excess.
3. On a lightly floured surface, roll cold dough into an 18x12-inch rectangle.
4. In a small bowl, whisk together Meyer lemon sugar and cardamom.
5. Using a pastry brush, brush remaining ¼ cup plus 2 tablespoons (85 grams) melted butter onto dough. Sprinkle lemon sugar mixture onto butter, leaving a ½-inch border along one long side. Starting at long side opposite border, roll up dough into a log. Trim edges if desired, and cut crosswise into 1-inch-thick slices.
6. Place slices, cut side up, in prepared muffin cups, gently pressing down until dough fills cups. Cover and let rise in a warm, draft-free place (75°F/24°C) until puffed, 45 minutes to 1 hour.
7. Preheat oven to 375°F (190°C).
8. Bake until golden brown and an instant-read thermometer inserted in center registers 210°F (99°C), 20 to 25 minutes, covering with foil halfway through baking to prevent excess browning if necessary. Let cool in pans for 10 minutes. Remove from pans, and dredge in blubeberry sugar. Serve warm.

Notes: *For Meyer lemon sugar, in the work bowl of a food processor, process 1 cup (200 grams) granulated sugar and 2 tablespoons (6 grams) Meyer lemon zest (about 2 lemons) until combined and uniform in color.*

For blueberry sugar, in the work bowl of a food processor, process 1 cup (200 grams) granulated sugar and ¼ cup (8 grams) freeze-dried blueberries until combined and uniform in color.

Everything Morning Buns

Makes 14 to 18 buns

This beauty goes to the savory side of breakfast, pairing crispy laminated texture with the savory flavor blend of everything bagel seasoning, sharp Cheddar, and cream cheese associated with the bagel. It's the mash-up you never knew you needed.

Danish Dough (recipe on page 102)
1½ teaspoons (7 grams) unsalted butter
¼ cup (34 grams) diced sweet onion
All-purpose flour, for dusting
4 ounces (113 grams) cream cheese, softened
1½ cups (150 grams) shredded sharp white Cheddar cheese
½ teaspoon garlic salt
Everything bagel seasoning, for sprinkling

1. Freeze Danish Dough for 15 to 30 minutes.
2. In a small skillet, melt butter over medium heat. Add onion; cook until soft and just starting to brown, 5 to 7 minutes. Let cool to room temperature.
3. Spray 14 to 18 muffin cups with cooking spray.
4. On a lightly floured surface, roll cold dough into an 18x12-inch rectangle. Spread cream cheese onto dough. Sprinkle onion, Cheddar, and garlic onto cream cheese, leaving a ½-inch border along one long edge. Starting at long side opposite border, roll up dough into a log. Trim edges if desired, and cut crosswise into 1-inch-thick slices.
5. Place slices, cut side up, in prepared muffin cups, gently pressing down until dough fills cups. Sprinkle with everything bagel seasoning. Cover and let rise in a warm, draft-free place (75°F/24°C) until puffed, 45 minutes to 1 hour.
6. Preheat oven to 375°F (190°C).
7. Bake until golden brown and an instant-read thermometer inserted in center registers 210°F (99°C), 20 to 25 minutes, covering with foil halfway through baking to prevent excess browning if necessary. Let cool in pans for 10 minutes. Serve warm.

Cranberry-Almond Kringle

Makes 2 kringles

Akin to an oversize Danish just begging to be sliced and shared, this is one bake that's sure to bring everyone together. In Denmark, the pastry is traditionally pretzel-shaped with an almond filling, also called *Wienerbrød* (Viennese bread). The *kringle* that's known and loved in the United States was first introduced in the 1800s by Danish immigrants moving to Wisconsin, namely in Racine.

1⅓ cups (303 grams) cold unsalted European-style butter, cubed
⅓ cup (80 grams) plus 1 tablespoon (15 grams) water, divided
6 tablespoons (72 grams) granulated sugar, divided
2¼ teaspoons (7 grams) active dry yeast
4½ cups (572 grams) bread flour
3½ teaspoons (10.5 grams) kosher salt
1 cup (240 grams) cold whole milk
All-purpose flour, for dusting
1 large egg (50 grams)
Almond Cream (recipe follows)
Quick Cranberry Jam (recipe follows)
Almond Glaze (recipe follows)

1. Freeze cold butter until firm, about 10 minutes.
2. In a small microwave-safe bowl, stir together ⅓ cup (80 grams) water and ½ teaspoon (2 grams) sugar; heat on high in 10-second intervals until an instant-read thermometer registers 110°F (43°C) to 115°F (46°C). Whisk in yeast until well combined. Let stand until foamy, 5 to 10 minutes.
3. In the bowl of a stand mixer fitted with the paddle attachment, beat bread flour, salt, and remaining 5 tablespoons plus 2½ teaspoons (70 grams) sugar at low speed until combined. Add ⅓ cup (76 grams) frozen butter; beat until mixture resembles coarse bread crumbs, about 3 minutes. Add remaining 1 cup (227 grams) frozen butter; pulse mixer between low speed and "off" just until butter is coated with flour.
4. Add cold milk to yeast mixture; while pulsing mixer between low speed and "off", add yeast mixture to flour mixture in a slow, steady stream just until a shaggy dough comes together. (There will still be large pieces of butter.) If any flour remains at bottom of bowl, gently knead by hand to incorporate.
5. Lightly dust work surface with all-purpose flour. Turn out dough onto prepared surface, and shape into a rough 7-inch square. (Dough will be soft and slightly sticky.) Wrap in plastic wrap, and freeze for 30 minutes.
6. Lightly dust work surface with all-purpose flour. On prepared surface, roll dough into an 18x9-inch rectangle, lightly dusting surface and top of dough as needed. Fold dough in half so short sides meet; lightly press dough at fold to mark center. Unfold dough. Fold short sides of dough to meet in center. Fold one half of dough onto other half of dough as if you are closing a book. (This is called a book-fold.) Rotate dough 90 degrees; repeat rolling and folding procedure. (Dough will start out soft, rough, and somewhat sticky but will come together; turn dough over as needed so edges are rolled out as evenly as possible.) Wrap in plastic wrap, and freeze for 15 minutes.
7. Repeat rolling and folding procedure once. (This will make a total of 3 book folds.) Wrap in plastic wrap, and refrigerate for at least 1½ hours or up to overnight.
8. Line 2 rimmed baking sheets with parchment paper.
9. In a small bowl, whisk together egg and remaining 1 tablespoon (15 grams) water.
10. Lightly dust work surface with all-purpose flour. Divide dough in half. On prepared surface, roll half of dough into a 26x9-inch rectangle. (Keep remaining dough refrigerated until ready to use.) (Dough will be thin. If at any point the dough is hard to roll out, cover with plastic wrap and let stand for 3 to 5 minutes before trying to roll again.) Gently score or mark dough in thirds lengthwise; you will have 3 (3-inch-wide) sections. Spread half of Almond Cream (scant ½ cup or 111 grams) down center third of rectangle, leaving a ¼-inch border at each short end. Spread half of Quick Cranberry Jam (⅓ cup or 111 grams) on top. Fold one side of dough over filling. Brush remaining side and ends of dough with egg wash, and fold over filling and

continued . . .

continued . . .

dough. Firmly press on all seams to make sure it seals. Make sure dough and filling are even, there are no air pockets, and it is still 26 inches long. Lift at both ends, and place on a prepared pan. Shape into an oval, making sure seam is at center of oval and not on outside edges, pressing ends together and pinching to seal. Oval should be even thickness and about 10x8 inches. Using a fork dipped in all-purpose flour, dock top of oval about every 1 inch. Cover and let rise in a warm, draft-free place (75°F/24°C) until puffed, about 30 minutes. Repeat with remaining dough, remaining Almond Cream, and remaining Quick Cranberry Jam when first kringle is ready to bake.

11. Preheat oven to 400°F (200°C).

12. Brush tops and sides with egg wash.

13. Bake until lightly browned, about 10 minutes. Reduce oven temperature to 350°F (180°C), and bake until golden brown and an instant-read thermometer inserted in pastry registers 190°F (88°C) to 200°F (93°C), 15 to 20 minutes more, covering with foil after 10 minutes of baking at 350°F (180°C) to prevent excess browning.

14. Increase oven temperature to 400°F (200°C). Repeat egg washing and baking with remaining kringle. Let cool completely on pans.

15. Spoon Almond Glaze onto cooled kringles. Store in an airtight container for up to 3 days.

Almond Cream

Makes about 1 cup

3 tablespoons (42 grams) unsalted butter, softened
¼ cup (50 grams) granulated sugar
⅔ cup (64 grams) almond flour
1 large egg white (30 grams)
⅛ teaspoon almond extract
¼ cup (31 grams) all-purpose flour
⅛ teaspoon kosher salt

1. In a medium bowl, beat butter and sugar with a hand mixer at medium speed until creamy, about 2 minutes, stopping to scrape sides of bowl. Beat in almond flour until well combined and no longer crumbly. Add egg white and extract; beat at low speed until combined. Beat in all-purpose flour and salt.

Quick Cranberry Jam

Makes about ⅔ cup

1 cup (100 grams) fresh or frozen cranberries
½ cup (100 grams) granulated sugar
½ teaspoon (1.5 grams) lightly packed orange zest
¼ cup (60 grams) fresh orange juice
½ teaspoon (1.5 grams) kosher salt
½ teaspoon (1 gram) ground cinnamon
2 tablespoons (30 grams) water
2 teaspoons (6 grams) cornstarch

1. In a medium saucepan, bring cranberries, sugar, orange zest and juice, salt, and cinnamon to a boil over medium heat. Reduce heat, and simmer, stirring occasionally, until cranberries are tender and burst and mixture thickens slightly, 5 to 8 minutes.

2. In a small bowl, whisk together 2 tablespoons (30 grams) water and cornstarch until dissolved. Whisk into cranberry mixture until well combined. Bring to a boil, whisking frequently. Cook for 2 minutes. Pour into a heatproof bowl, and let cool completely before using.

Almond Glaze

Makes 1 cup

1 cup (120 grams) confectioners' sugar
2 tablespoons plus 2 teaspoons (40 grams) water
2 tablespoons (28 grams) unsalted butter, melted
¼ teaspoon kosher salt
⅛ teaspoon almond extract

1. In a medium bowl, whisk together confectioners' sugar, 2 tablespoons plus 2 teaspoons (40 grams) water, melted butter, salt, and almond extract until smooth. Use immediately.

Preparing the Dough

Keeping your dough cold throughout mixing and shaping will ensure the butter holds its shape, ultimately creating this bake's signature laminated layering

Freeze cold butter until firm, about 10 minutes.

In a small microwave-safe bowl, stir together ⅓ cup (80 grams) water and ½ teaspoon (2 grams) sugar; heat on high in 10-second intervals until an instant-read thermometer registers 110°F (43°C) to 115°F (46°C). Whisk in yeast until well combined. Let stand until foamy, 5 to 10 minutes.

In the bowl of a stand mixer fitted with the paddle attachment, beat bread flour, salt, and remaining 5 tablespoons plus 2½ teaspoons (70 grams) sugar at low speed until combined. Add ⅓ cup (76 grams) frozen butter; beat until mixture resembles coarse bread crumbs, about 3 minutes. Add remaining 1 cup (227 grams) frozen butter; pulse mixer between low speed and "off" just until butter is coated with flour.

TIP: It's important not to overmix at this stage. Larger pieces of butter will help to create more defined layers as the dough is rolled out and laminated.

Add cold milk to yeast mixture; while pulsing mixer between low speed and "off," add yeast mixture to flour mixture in a slow, steady stream just until a shaggy dough comes together. (There will still be large pieces of butter.) If any flour remains at bottom of bowl, gently knead by hand to incorporate.

Lightly dust work surface with all-purpose flour. Turn out dough, and shape into a rough 7-inch square. (Dough will be soft and slightly sticky.) Wrap in plastic wrap, and freeze for 30 minutes.

Folding the Dough

Lightly dust work surface with all-purpose flour. Roll dough into an 18x9-inch rectangle, lightly dusting surface and top of dough with all-purpose flour as needed. Fold dough in half so short sides meet; lightly press dough at fold to mark center. Unfold dough. Fold short sides of dough to meet in center. Fold one half of dough onto other half of dough as if you are closing a book. (This is called a book-fold.) Rotate dough 90 degrees; repeat rolling and folding procedure. (Dough will start out soft, rough, and somewhat sticky but will come together; turn dough over as needed so edges are rolled out as evenly as possible.) Wrap in plastic wrap, and freeze for 15 minutes.

TIP: Freezing in between folds will help keep your butter cold. If at any point you notice your butter melting, return the dough to the freezer to allow it to firm up.

Repeat rolling and folding procedure. (This will make a total of 3 book-folds.) Wrap in plastic wrap, and refrigerate for at least 1½ hours or up to overnight.

Filling and Shaping

The most important part of shaping your kringles is ensuring that all seams are sealed to prevent any filling from spilling out as they bake. Egg wash and crimping will help create a sturdy seal.

Line 2 rimmed baking sheets with parchment paper.

In a small bowl, whisk together egg and 1 tablespoon (15 grams) water.

Lightly dust work surface with all-purpose flour. Divide dough in half. Roll half of dough into a 26x9-inch rectangle. (Keep remaining dough refrigerated until ready to use.) (Dough will be thin. If at any point the dough is hard to roll out, cover with plastic wrap, and let stand for 3 to 5 minutes before trying to roll again.) Gently score or mark dough in thirds lengthwise; you will have 3 (3-inch-wide) sections. **TIP:** These lines will act as a guide for your filling and folds. It's important that you don't cut through your dough, otherwise your filling might leak out when you shape or bake your kringles.

Spread half of Almond Cream (scant ½ cup or 111 grams) down center third of rectangle, leaving a ¼-inch border at each short end. Top with half of Quick Cranberry Jam (⅓ cup or 111 grams).

Fold one side of dough over filling. Brush remaining side and ends of dough with egg wash, and fold over filling and dough. Firmly press all seams to make sure it seals. Make sure dough and filling are even, there are no air pockets, and it is still 26 inches long. Lift at both ends, and place on a prepared pan. Shape into an oval, making sure seam is at center of oval and not on outside edges, pressing ends together and pinching to seal. Oval should be even thickness and about 10x8 inches. Using a fork dipped in flour, dock top of oval about every 1 inch. Cover and let rise in a warm, draft-free place (75°F/24°C) until puffed, about 30 minutes. Repeat with remaining dough, remaining Almond Cream, and remaining Quick Cranberry Jam when first kringle is ready to bake.

Preheat oven to 400°F (200°C).

Brush tops and sides of dough with egg wash.

Bake until dough is lightly browned, about 10 minutes. Reduce oven temperature to 350°F (180°C), and bake until golden brown and an instant-read thermometer inserted in pastry registers 190°F (88°C) to 200°F (93°C), 15 to 20 minutes more, covering with foil after 10 minutes of baking at 350°F (180°C) to prevent excess browning.

Increase oven temperature to 400°F (200°C). Repeat egg washing and baking with remaining kringle.

Brioche Dough

This buttery beauty is the base for brioche of many shapes and sizes and bakes into an ultra-soft, slightly sweet crumb that shines. Its golden hue and fluffy interior are simply irresistible, and it'll be nearly impossible not to devour it the minute your bread emerges from the oven.

- ⅓ cup (80 grams) warm whole milk (110°F/43°C to 115°F/46°C)
- 2¼ teaspoons (7 grams) instant yeast
- 3 tablespoons (36 grams) granulated sugar, divided
- 2⅓ to 2⅔ cups (292 to 334 grams) all-purpose flour, divided, plus more for dusting
- 2 teaspoons (6 grams) kosher salt
- 2 large eggs (100 grams), lightly beaten and room temperature
- ½ cup (113 grams) unsalted butter, cubed and room temperature

1. In a small bowl, stir together warm milk, yeast, and 1 teaspoon (4 grams) sugar. Let stand until foamy, about 5 minutes.

2. In the bowl of a stand mixer, whisk together 1⅓ cups (167 grams) flour, salt, and remaining 2 tablespoons plus 2 teaspoons (32 grams) sugar. Add yeast mixture and eggs. Using the paddle attachment, beat at low speed until combined, about 1 minute. With mixer on low speed, gradually add 1 cup (125 grams) flour, beating until a shaggy dough forms; scrape sides of bowl.

3. Switch to the dough hook attachment. Beat at medium-low speed until dough is smooth, elastic, and slightly tacky, 4 to 6 minutes; add up to remaining ⅓ cup (42 grams) flour, 1 tablespoon (8 grams) at a time, if dough is too sticky. With mixer on medium-low speed, add butter, 1 tablespoon (14 grams) at a time, beating until combined after each addition (6 to 7 minutes total). Beat at medium speed until a smooth, elastic dough forms, 10 to 12 minutes. Turn out onto a lightly floured surface; knead 5 to 8 times, and shape into a smooth round.

4. Lightly oil a large bowl. Place dough in bowl, turning to grease top. Cover and let rise in a warm, draft-free place (75°F/24°C) until doubled in size, 45 minutes to 1 hour.

5. Line a baking sheet with parchment paper.

6. Turn out dough onto a lightly floured surface, and lightly punch down dough. Flatten dough into an 8x6-inch rectangle, and transfer to prepared pan. Cover with plastic wrap, and refrigerate for at least 8 hours or up to overnight.

pro tip

Unlike softened butter, room temperature butter is warm enough to easily incorporate into your dough and should have no resistance when pressed with a finger.

Brioche: All About the Butter

It adds so much more than flavor

Unsalted European-style butter adds unmatched flavor, texture, and depth to brioche. The butter sits at about 34% of the flour weight, making for an incredibly rich, tender dough. You'll notice that butter is the last ingredient added in this recipe, and that's for good reason. Fats like butter slow down the gluten-forming process, which is part of the reason why enriched breads typically call for a longer mixing time. The fat in the butter coats protein strands, acting like a barrier that prevents gluten proteins from sticking to one another, inhibiting the growth of long chains that ultimately create the bread's feathery texture. So, it's important that gluten structures are already formed before the butter is added; otherwise, you won't get brioche's distinct, pull-apart texture.

Making the Dough

This egg- and butter-rich dough is all about ingredient temperature, which allows for proper gluten development and ample rise time. Enriched breads have a long proof time, so patience is key.

In a small bowl, stir together warm milk, yeast, and 1 teaspoon (4 grams) sugar. Let stand until foamy, about 5 minutes.

TIP: This step, also known as blooming the yeast, is a simple way to ensure that your yeast is active and is going to work. If it isn't foamy after 5 minutes, you'll want to start over with new yeast. Also, keep in mind that yeast is killed at 140°F (60°C), so keep your thermometer on hand when heating the milk.

In the bowl of a stand mixer, whisk together 1⅓ cups (167 grams) flour, salt, and remaining 2 tablespoons plus 2 teaspoons (32 grams) sugar. Add yeast mixture and eggs. Using the paddle attachment, beat at low speed until combined, about 1 minute. With mixer on low speed, gradually add 1 cup (125 grams) flour, beating until a shaggy dough forms; scrape sides of bowl.

Switch to the dough hook attachment. Beat at medium-low speed until dough is smooth, elastic, and slightly tacky, 4 to 6 minutes; add up to remaining ⅓ cup (42 grams) flour, 1 tablespoon (8 grams) at a time, if dough is too sticky. With mixer on medium-low speed, add butter, 1 tablespoon (14 grams) at a time, beating until combined after each addition (6 to 7 minutes total).

TIP: As the butter is incorporated, friction and heat from the mixer will warm it, so it's important that the butter not be too soft; otherwise, it may melt and separate from the dough. Conversely, if the butter is too cold, it won't incorporate smoothly into the dough and chunks of butter will remain even after mixing. For this reason, it's important that your butter is added into your dough at true room temperature. Don't panic if the butter doesn't incorporate immediately; go slow and only add more once it's fully incorporated.

Beat at medium speed until a smooth, elastic dough forms, 10 to 12 minutes.

TIP: When done mixing, the dough should be soft without being sticky.

Turn out onto a lightly floured surface; knead 5 to 8 times, and shape into a smooth round. Lightly oil a large bowl. Place dough in bowl, turning to grease top. Cover and let rise in a warm, draft-free place (75°F/24°C) until doubled in size, 45 minutes to 1 hour.

Line a baking sheet with parchment paper. Turn out dough onto a lightly floured surface, and lightly punch down dough. Flatten dough into an 8x6-inch rectangle, and transfer to prepared pan. Cover with plastic wrap, and refrigerate for at least 8 hours or up to overnight.

TIP: A proof in the refrigerator allows for more fermentation time, which ultimately results in a more flavorful brioche. Enriched doughs are notorious for taking a longer time to rise, so patience is key. Your waiting will be rewarded.

Brioche Loaf

Makes 1 (8½x4½-inch) loaf

This sweet and simple loaf gets its gorgeous bubbly top from a simple braid. With braided breads, it's important that the ends are sealed and not tucked or folded under the loaf; otherwise, it may rise and bake slightly misshapen.

All-purpose flour, for dusting
Brioche Dough (recipe on page 120)
1 large egg (50 grams)
1 tablespoon (15 grams) water

1. Lightly spray an 8½x4½-inch loaf pan with baking spray with flour. Line pan with parchment paper, letting excess extend over sides of pan.
2. On a lightly floured surface, divide Brioche Dough into 3 portions (about 217 grams each). Roll each portion into a rope about 14 inches long. Pinch ropes together at one end, and carefully braid together tightly. Pinch ends to seal. Place braid in prepared pan, compressing to fit as needed. (Try not to fold the dough too much under itself; this will result in an irregular bumpy top.)
3. Cover and let rise in a warm, draft-free place (75°F/24°C) until puffed and dough passes the finger dent test, 50 to 55 minutes. (See Note.)
4. Preheat oven to 350°F (180°C).
5. In a small bowl, whisk together egg and 1 tablespoon (15 grams) water; lightly brush onto dough.
6. Bake until golden brown and an instant-read thermometer inserted in center registers 190°F (88°C), 40 to 45 minutes, covering with foil during final 15 minutes of baking to prevent excess browning. Let cool in pan for 10 minutes. Using excess parchment as handles, remove from pan, and let cool completely on a wire rack. Store in an airtight container for up to 3 days.

Note: *To use the finger dent test, lightly flour the surface of the dough, and gently press your finger about ½ inch into the surface. If your dough has properly fermented, you should be able to watch the dough spring back slightly but still show an indentation. If the dent disappears, the dough is underproofed and needs more time.*

Shaping Success

Keeping this dough cold will make shaping far less stress-inducing (another bonus of having the dough complete its second rise in the refrigerator). All the butter becomes quite messy if your dough gets too warm from handling, so try to work quickly and efficiently.

If the dough is not rolling out easily and, instead, snapping back into place every time you try to shape it, cover the dough, let it rest for 10 to 15 minutes, and then try again. This allows the gluten to rest and let go of some tension, making it much easier to work with.

To roll out each piece, apply even pressure with both hands flat, rolling dough toward and away from you, moving hands outward as you press.

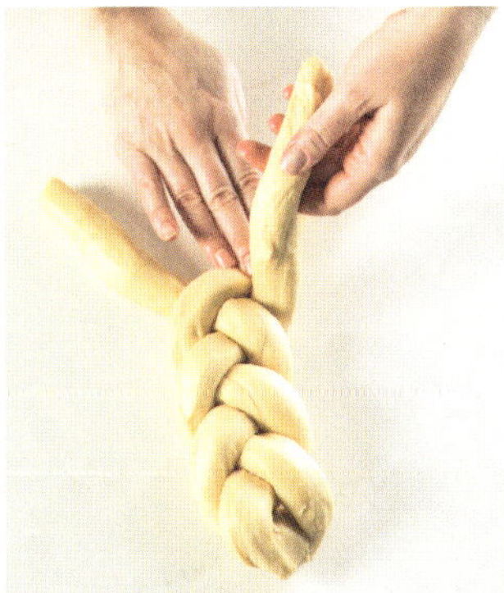

Make sure both ends are well sealed; otherwise, the dough may expand and come undone as it rises and bakes.

Place braid in prepared pan, compressing to fit as needed. Try not to fold the dough too much under itself; this will result in an irregular bumpy top.

Brioche au Sucre

Makes 6 buns

Formed into rounds and then coated with egg wash and Swedish pearl sugar, these buns are as beautiful as they are delicious. Their shaping is straightforward, but pay attention to the seams and make sure each round is properly sealed.

Brioche Dough (recipe on page 120)
1 large egg (50 grams)
1 tablespoon (15 grams) water
Swedish pearl sugar, for sprinkling

1. Line a baking sheet with parchment paper.
2. Divide Brioche Dough into 6 portions (about 103 grams each). Shape each into a tight round, folding dough in on itself to create a smooth top and gathering edges into one seam. Place, seam side down, on a clean surface, and using a cupped hand, pull dough toward you. Rotate dough 90 degrees, and repeat until you have a smooth, tight, and sealed round.
3. Place at least 2 inches apart on prepared pan. Cover and let rise in a warm, draft-free place (75°F/24°C) until puffed, 45 minutes to 1 hour.
4. Preheat oven to 350°F (180°C).
5. In a small bowl, whisk together egg and 1 tablespoon (15 grams) water; lightly brush onto buns. Sprinkle with pearl sugar.
6. Bake until golden brown and an instant-read thermometer inserted in center registers 190°F (88°C), 25 to 30 minutes. Let cool on pan for 15 minutes. Remove from pan, and let cool completely on a wire rack. Store in an airtight container for up to 3 days.

Shaping Success

The pulling and rotating motion is what seals the seams of the bun, so make sure you're applying gentle pressure as you pull, taking advantage of the resistance the counter provides. Place at least 2 inches apart on prepared pan.

Pain Suisse

Makes 8 pastries

Brioche dough creates buttery bookends for a vanilla bean seed- and chocolate chip-dotted custard. Orange zest adds a touch of citrus to the dough, and a brushing of floral orange blossom syrup keeps the bread rich and moist for days.

⅓ cup (80 grams) warm whole milk (110°F/43°C to 115°F/46°C)
1½ teaspoons (4.5 grams) instant yeast
6 teaspoons (24 grams) granulated sugar, divided
2 to 2⅓ cups (250 to 292 grams) all-purpose flour, divided, plus more for dusting
2 teaspoons (6 grams) kosher salt
1 teaspoon (3 grams) tightly packed orange zest (about 1 medium orange)
3 large eggs (150 grams), room temperature and divided
⅓ cup (76 grams) unsalted butter, cubed and room temperature
Vanilla Bean Pastry Cream (recipe follows)
⅓ cup (61 grams) mini semisweet chocolate chips
1 tablespoon (15 grams) water
Orange Blossom Simple Syrup (recipe follows)

1. In a small bowl, stir together warm milk, yeast, and 1 teaspoon (4 grams) sugar. Let stand until foamy, about 5 minutes.
2. In the bowl of a stand mixer, whisk together 2 cups (250 grams) flour, salt, orange zest, and remaining 5 teaspoons (20 grams) sugar. Add yeast mixture and 2 eggs (100 grams); using the paddle attachment, beat at low speed until a shaggy dough forms, about 1 minute; scrape sides of bowl.
3. Switch to the dough hook attachment. Beat at medium-low speed until dough is smooth, elastic, and slightly tacky, about 15 minutes; add up to remaining ⅓ cup (42 grams) flour, 1 tablespoon (8 grams) at a time, if dough is too sticky. With mixer on medium-low speed, add butter, 1 tablespoon (14 grams) at a time, beating until combined after each addition (7 to 8 minutes total). Beat until a smooth, elastic dough forms, 12 to 14 minutes. Turn out dough onto a lightly floured surface, and knead 5 to 8 times. Shape dough into a smooth round.
4. Lightly oil a large bowl. Place dough in bowl, turning to grease top. Cover and let rise in a warm, draft-free place (75°F/24°C) until doubled in size, 45 minutes to 1 hour. Refrigerate for at least 1 hour or up to overnight.
5. Line 2 rimmed baking sheets with parchment paper.
6. Whisk Vanilla Bean Pastry Cream until smooth.
7. Lightly punch down dough. Cover and let stand for 5 minutes. On a lightly floured surface, gently roll dough into a 12x10-inch rectangle, one long side closest to you. Using a knife or offset spatula, evenly spread Vanilla Bean Pastry Cream onto dough, leaving a ½-inch border along on long sides. Sprinkle chocolate chips ont bottom half of pastry cream, and gently press with your hand to completely adhere chocolate to pastry cream. Fold top half of dough over to cover pastry cream and chocolate. Lightly press seam to seal. Using a long knife or pastry wheel, cut into 8 (5x1½-inch) strips. Place strips 2 inches apart on prepared pans. Loosely cover and let rise in a warm, draft-free place (75°F/24°C) until puffed, 45 to 55 minutes.
8. Preheat oven to 350°F (180°C).
9. In a small bowl, gently whisk together 1 tablespoon (15 grams) water and remaining 1 egg (50 grams). Lightly brush egg wash over dough.
10. Bake until tops are golden brown and an instant-read thermometer inserted in center registers 190°F (88°C), 30 to 35 minutes. Using a pastry brush, immediately brush a thin layer of Orange Blossom Simple Syrup onto pastries. Let cool on pans for 10 minutes. Serve warm, or remove from pans, and let cool completely on a wire rack. Refrigerate in an airtight container for up to 3 days.

Vanilla Bean Pastry Cream

Makes 1 cup

- ¾ **cup plus 2 tablespoons (210 grams) whole milk**
- 4 **tablespoons (48 grams) granulated sugar, divided**
- 1 **teaspoon (6 grams) vanilla bean paste**
- ⅛ **teaspoon kosher salt**
- 3 **large egg yolks (56 grams), room temperature**
- 5 **teaspoons (15 grams) cornstarch**
- 1 **tablespoon (14 grams) unsalted butter, cubed**

1. In a small saucepan, heat milk, 2 tablespoons (24 grams) sugar, vanilla bean paste, and salt over medium heat, stirring occasionally, until steaming. (Do not boil.)

2. In a medium bowl, whisk together egg yolks, cornstarch, and remaining 2 tablespoons (24 grams) sugar. Add hot milk mixture, whisking constantly. Pour egg mixture into saucepan; cook over medium heat, whisking constantly, until mixture starts to boil. Cook, whisking constantly, until thickened, 2 to 3 minutes.

3. Remove from heat, and strain through a fine-mesh sieve into a medium heatproof bowl. Stir in butter until completely combined. Cover with plastic wrap, pressing wrap directly onto surface of pastry cream to prevent a skin from forming. Refrigerate until thick and cold, at least 4 hours, or overnight. Whisk well before using.

Orange Blossom Simple Syrup

Makes ⅓ cup

- ¼ **cup (50 grams) granulated sugar**
- 3 **tablespoons (45 grams) water**
- 2 **teaspoons (10 grams) orange blossom water**

4. In a small saucepan, heat sugar, 3 tablespoons (45 grams) water, and orange blossom water over medium heat, whisking occasionally, until sugar dissolves, about 4 minutes. Let cool completely.

Pain au Raisin Sweet Rolls

Makes 6 rolls

Baked to tall, golden perfection in copper soufflé molds, these spirals are a home baker-friendly version of the pâtissière original, with a simple frangipane filling replacing pastry cream.

3½ tablespoons (52.5 grams) warm whole milk (105°F/41°C to 110°F/43°C)
3½ tablespoons (42 grams) granulated sugar, divided
1¼ teaspoons (3.75 grams) active dry yeast
2 cups (250 grams) all-purpose flour, divided, plus more for dusting
3 large eggs (150 grams), room temperature
½ teaspoon (1.5 grams) kosher salt
9 tablespoons (126 grams) unsalted butter, softened
⅔ cup (114 grams) raisins
⅓ cup (60 grams) golden raisins
3 tablespoons (45 grams) warm brandy
1 tablespoon (14 grams) unsalted butter, melted
Frangipane (recipe follows)
1 large egg white (30 grams)
2 tablespoons (30 grams) water, divided
Swedish pearl sugar, for sprinkling
⅓ cup (107 grams) apricot preserves

1. In the bowl of a stand mixer fitted with the paddle attachment, combine warm milk, 1 tablespoon (12 grams) granulated sugar, and yeast. Let stand until mixture is foamy, about 10 minutes. Add 1 cup (125 grams) flour and eggs; beat at medium-low speed until mostly smooth, 2 to 3 minutes, stopping to scrape sides of bowl. (Some small lumps remaining are OK.) Cover and let stand in a warm, draft-free place (75°F/24°C) until slightly puffed with small bubbles forming over top and at edges, 30 to 45 minutes.
2. Switch to the dough hook attachment. Add salt, remaining 1 cup (125 grams) flour, and remaining 2½ tablespoons (30 grams) granulated sugar; beat at low speed just until combined. Increase mixer speed to medium, and beat until dough is smooth and elastic, 7 to 10 minutes, stopping to scrape sides of bowl.
3. With mixer on medium-low speed, add softened butter, 1 tablespoon (14 grams) at a time, beating until combined after each addition. (Dough should pass the windowpane test; see note on page 89.)
4. Spray a large bowl with cooking spray. Place dough in bowl, turning to grease top. Cover and let rise in a warm, draft-free place (75°F/24°C) until doubled in size, 45 minutes to 1 hour.
5. On a lightly floured surface, turn out dough; fold dough 4 to 6 times to knock out air. Return dough to bowl; cover and refrigerate for at least 5 hours or up to 8 hours. (You can also do an overnight proof for a maximum of 12 hours. Make sure to place the dough in a large bowl, giving it room to grow.)
6. In a medium bowl, combine all raisins and warm brandy; let stand for 20 minutes.
7. Line a rimmed baking sheet with parchment paper. Using a pastry brush, coat 6 (3-inch) copper soufflé molds (see Note) with melted butter, using vertical strokes up sides. Flour molds, shaking out excess. Place molds on prepared pan.
8. Turn out dough onto a heavily floured surface; lightly flour top of dough. Roll dough into a 16x10-inch rectangle. Using a small offset spatula, dot Frangipane onto dough; spread into an even layer, leaving a ½-inch border on one long side. Sprinkle soaked raisins onto Frangipane. Starting at side without border, roll dough into a 16-inch log. Gently shape log with hands to right length and more even thickness, if necessary. Using a serrated knife dipped in flour, cut log into 6 (2½-inch-thick) slices, trimming ends if necessary. Place slices, cut side down, in prepared molds. Loosely cover and let rise in a warm, draft-free place (75°F/24°C) until dough springs back when touched, 20 to 35 minutes.
9. Preheat oven to 350°F (180°C).
10. In a small bowl, whisk together egg white and 1 tablespoon (15 grams) water. Using a pastry brush, brush egg wash onto rolls; sprinkle with pearl sugar.
11. Bake until golden brown and an instant-read thermometer inserted in center registers 190°F (88°C), 20 to 30 minutes. Let cool in molds for 5 minutes. Carefully remove from molds, and place on a wire rack.
12. In a small microwave-safe bowl, heat preserves and remaining 1 tablespoon (15 grams) water on high in 10-second intervals, stirring between each, until

melted. Strain mixture through a fine-mesh sieve, discarding solids. Brush onto rolls. Serve warm.

Note: *This recipe also works in tall (2 inch-high) 8-ounce ramekins or jumbo muffin cups.*

Frangipane

Makes about 1½ cups

- **7 tablespoons (98 grams) unsalted butter, room temperature**
- **1 cup (96 grams) very finely ground almond flour**
- **½ cup (100 grams) granulated sugar**
- **1 large egg (50 grams)**
- **2½ tablespoons (20 grams) all-purpose flour**
- **¾ teaspoon (2.25 grams) kosher salt**
- **¾ teaspoon (3 grams) almond extract**

1. In a medium bowl, whisk butter until creamy. Whisk in all remaining ingredients until smooth and well combined. Use immediately, or cover with a piece of plastic wrap, pressing wrap directly onto surface of paste to prevent a skin from forming, and refrigerate for up to 3 days. Heat cold Frangipane in microwave-safe bowl in 5-second intervals just until spreadable.

German Sour Cream Twists

Makes 24 twists

Sour cream adds a hint of tanginess to these classic German pastries.

- 1½ cups (300 grams) granulated sugar
- 1 vanilla bean, halved lengthwise, seeds scraped and reserved
- ¼ cup (60 grams) warm water (105°F/41°C to 110°F/43°C)
- 2¼ teaspoons (7 grams) instant yeast
- 3¾ cups (469 grams) all-purpose flour
- 1 cup (227 grams) cold unsalted butter, cubed
- ¾ teaspoon (2.25 grams) kosher salt
- ¾ cup (180 grams) sour cream, room temperature
- 2 large eggs (100 grams), room temperature
- 1 teaspoon (4 grams) vanilla extract

1. In a medium bowl, place sugar and vanilla bean halves and reserved seeds. Using your fingers, rub vanilla into sugar until well combined. Cover and reserve.

2. In a small bowl, stir together ¼ cup (60 grams) warm water and yeast. Let stand until foamy, about 5 minutes.

3. In the bowl of a stand mixer fitted with the paddle attachment, beat flour, cold butter, and salt at low speed until mixture resembles coarse crumbs, 3 to 5 minutes. Beat in yeast mixture, sour cream, eggs, and vanilla extract until well combined and a sticky dough forms. Cover and refrigerate for at least 2 hours or overnight.

4. Preheat oven to 375°F (190°C). Line baking sheets with parchment paper.

5. Divide dough in half (about 513 grams each); cover and refrigerate one portion. Sprinkle ¼ cup (50 grams) vanilla sugar on work surface. On prepared surface, roll dough into a 12x8-inch rectangle. Sprinkle 2 tablespoons (24 grams) vanilla sugar onto dough; fold dough into thirds like a letter. Rotatoe dough 90 degrees; repeat rolling, sprinkling, and folding two more times. (If dough sticks in spots during rolling process, sprinkle vanilla sugar as if it were flour.) Roll into a 12x8-inch rectangle, and cut into 12 (1-inch-wide) strips. Twist each strip 3 to 4 times. Place 2 inches apart on prepared pans, and refrigerate. Repeat procedure with remaining dough.

6. Bake, one pan at a time, until golden brown, 15 to 20 minutes. Let cool on pan for 5 minutes. Remove from pan, and let cool completely on a wire rack. Store in an airtight container for up to 3 days.

pâte à choux

choux pastry dough

ÉCLAIRS, CREAM PUFFS, GOUGÈRES

The high moisture content in choux pastry creates a high, domed rise as it bakes, which results in a golden-brown exterior and an airy, almost hollow interior. Choux pastry can also be fried to create decadent dredged and glazed doughnuts.

Choux Pastry Dough

Choux pastry harnesses the power of steam rather than leavening to rise. While baking, the outside sets, with the fat crisping into a golden exterior. Inside, the trapped air pockets combine and expand into one perfect bubble.

½ cup (113 grams) unsalted butter, cubed
½ cup (120 grams) water
½ cup (120 grams) whole milk
2 teaspoons (8 grams) granulated sugar
1 teaspoon (3 grams) kosher salt
1 cup (125 grams) all-purpose flour
5 large eggs (250 grams), room temperature

1. In a medium saucepan, bring butter, ½ cup (120 grams) water, milk, sugar, and salt to a rolling boil over medium-high heat. Using a wooden spoon, stir in flour. Cook, stirring constantly, until a skin forms on bottom of pan and mixture pulls away from sides of pan and forms a ball, 2 to 3 minutes.
2. Transfer mixture to the bowl of a stand mixer fitted with the paddle attachment; beat at low speed until dough cools slightly, 3 to 4 minutes. Add eggs, one at a time, beating until smooth and combined after each addition. (Dough will be shiny and will slowly move back together when a spatula is dragged through it.)

From Stovetop to Stand Mixer

In a medium saucepan, bring butter, water, milk, granulated sugar, and salt to a rolling boil over medium-high heat.
TIP: Be sure to cube the butter before adding it to the other ingredients. If you add whole sticks of butter, the butter will take too long to melt and too much water will evaporate while bringing to a boil.

Add flour, and using a wooden spoon, stir until combined. Cook, stirring constantly, until a skin forms on bottom of pan and mixture pulls away from sides of pan and forms a ball.
TIP: As you stir, make sure to remove lingering flour pockets. You're essentially cooking off the excess moisture and the raw flour flavor. It should go from looking like mashed potatoes to congealing into a paste-like dough.

Transfer mixture to the bowl of a stand mixer fitted with the paddle attachment; beat at low speed until dough cools slightly.
TIP: This helps cool down the dough a bit before adding in your eggs.

Add eggs, one at a time, beating until combined after each addition. Dough will be shiny and will slowly move back together when a spatula is dragged through it; batter should also fall off paddle so excess is left hanging in a "V" shape.
TIP: When beating in the eggs, your dough might look broken at first, but it will eventually come together. Beyond using a spatula to test your dough, the paddle attachment can be used to conduct the "V" shape test as well.

Perfect Piping

Line baking sheets with parchment paper. Using a permanent marker, draw circles or lines about 2 inches apart on a sheet of parchment paper. Slide template under parchment on a prepared pan.

TIP: You'll want to bake the choux one pan at a time so they can bake evenly. The parchment paper template is your guide when piping.

Transfer dough to a large pastry bag fitted with a small piping tip.

TIP: For a mess-free dough transfer, place pastry bag in a large jar or glass and fold the bag edges over the rim of the glass before spooning in the dough.

For round shapes, place piping tip in center of a drawn circle. Hold tip perpendicular ½ inch above parchment paper.

Holding tip stationary the entire time, apply even pressure until dough reaches edges of drawn circle. Stop applying pressure, and move tip in a quick circular motion as you lift away to help prevent a point from forming on top.

For long shapes, hold tip about ¾ inch above parchment, and slowly pipe out dough. Ease up on pressure at end of line; stop, and lift up. Smooth end of dough with a damp fingertip.

Repeat with remaining dough until pan is full. Wet your finger with water, and press down any points to create a smooth top, if necessary.

Choux au Craquelin

Makes about 18 pastries

These crisp sugar cookie-capped Choux au Craquelin are one of the sweetest examples of what choux can bring to the table. With hollow interiors generously filled with fluffy vanilla cream, these choux are a triumph of French pâtisserie.

Choux Pastry Dough (recipe on page 136)
Craquelin Cookies (recipe follows)
Diplomat Cream (recipe follows)

1. Preheat oven to 375°F (190°C). Line 2 to 3 baking sheets with parchment paper.
2. Using a permanent marker and a 2-inch round cutter as a guide, draw circles at least 1½ inches apart on another sheet of parchment paper; slide template under parchment on a prepared pan.
3. Transfer Choux Pastry Dough to a large pastry bag fitted with a ½-inch round piping tip (Ateco #807). Place piping tip in center of a drawn circle. Holding tip perpendicularly ½ inch above parchment paper and stationary the entire time, apply even pressure until batter reaches edges of drawn circle. Stop applying pressure, and move tip in a quick circular motion as you lift away to help prevent a point from forming on top. Repeat with remaining batter until pan is full.
4. Wet your finger with water, and press down any points to create a smooth top, if necessary. Slide template out from under piped batter, and place under parchment on other prepared pans; pipe remaining batter.
5. Top each piped choux puff with a frozen Craquelin Cookie right before baking.
6. Bake, one pan at a time, for 10 minutes. Rotate pan, and bake until fully puffed and deep golden brown, 10 to 15 minutes more. Let cool completely on pans.
7. Using a serrated knife, cut off top quarter of each cooled choux puff; reserve. Using a skewer or wooden pick, clear any dough strands.
8. Place Diplomat Cream in a large pastry bag fitted with a ½-inch open star piping tip (Ateco #826). Pipe cream into each puff, and place cut top piece on top of piped cream. Serve immediately, or cover and refrigerate until ready to serve. Best served same day as made.

Craquelin Cookies

Makes about 18 cookies

½ cup (75 grams) all-purpose flour
⅓ cup (73 grams) firmly packed light brown sugar
⅛ teaspoon kosher salt
¼ cup (57 grams) cold unsalted butter, cubed

1. In the work bowl of a food processor, pulse flour, brown sugar, and salt until combined. Add cold butter, and process until mixture starts to clump together, about 30 seconds. Pulse until large clumps form and mixture sticks together when pinched, 5 to 6 pulses.
2. Turn out dough onto a clean work surface, and knead 2 to 3 times to bring together. Press into a disk. Place dough between 2 pieces of parchment paper, and roll to ⅛-inch thickness. Place on a baking sheet, and freeze until firm, 20 to 30 minutes.
3. Using a 1¾-inch round cutter, cut dough. Reroll scraps between parchment, and freeze for 10 minutes before cutting more disks. Freeze disks on a baking sheet or in a resealable plastic bag until ready to use.

Diplomat Cream

Makes about 4¼ cups

1¼ cups (300 grams) whole milk
6 tablespoons (72 grams) granulated sugar, divided
¼ teaspoon kosher salt
3 large egg yolks (56 grams), room temperature
3 tablespoons (24 grams) cornstarch
1 tablespoon (14 grams) unsalted butter, cubed
1½ teaspoons (9 grams) vanilla bean paste or (6 grams) vanilla extract
1½ cups (360 grams) cold heavy whipping cream

Top each piped choux puff with a frozen Craquelin Cookie right before baking.

1. In a medium saucepan, heat milk, 3 tablespoons (36 grams) sugar, and salt over medium heat, stirring occasionally, until steaming. (Do not boil.)

2. In a medium bowl, whisk together egg yolks, cornstarch, and remaining 3 tablespoons (36 grams) sugar until smooth. Gradually add hot milk mixture, whisking constantly. Pour egg mixture into saucepan, and bring to a boil over medium-low heat, whisking constantly. Cook, whisking constantly, until bubbly and thickened, 2 to 3 minutes.

3. Strain mixture through a fine-mesh sieve into a medium heatproof bowl, discarding solids. Whisk in butter until melted and well combined; whisk in vanilla. Cover with plastic wrap, pressing wrap directly onto surface of pastry cream to prevent a skin from forming. Refrigerate until thick and cold, at least 4 hours, or up to overnight.

4. In the bowl of a stand mixer fitted with the whisk attachment, beat cold cream at medium-low speed until foamy. Increase mixer speed to medium-high, and beat until stiff peaks form.

5. Whisk cold pastry cream until smooth. Fold in half of whipped cream until a few white streaks remain. Fold in remaining whipped cream just until combined. Use immediately, or refrigerate until ready to use. Best used same day as made.

Chouquettes

Makes about 30 pastries

A sprinkle of pearl sugar provides the perfect crunch to these airy little puffs, which are pronounced "shoo-keht."

Choux Pastry Dough (recipe on page 136)
1 large egg (50 grams), beaten
Swedish pearl sugar, for sprinkling

1. Preheat oven to 375°F (190°C). Line 2 to 3 baking sheets with parchment paper.
2. Using a permanent marker and a 1½-inch round cutter as a guide, draw circles 2 inches apart on another sheet of parchment paper; slide template under parchment on a prepared pan.
3. Transfer Choux Pastry Dough to a large pastry bag fitted with a ½-inch round piping tip (Ateco #805). Place piping tip in center of a drawn circle. Holding tip perpendicularly ½ inch above parchment paper and stationary the entire time, apply even pressure until batter reaches edges of drawn circle. Stop applying pressure, and move tip in a quick circular motion as you lift away to help prevent a point from forming on top. Repeat with remaining batter until pan is full.
4. Wet your finger with water, and press down any points to create a smooth top, if necessary. Slide template out from under piped batter, and place under parchment on other prepared pans; pipe remaining batter.
5. Using a pastry brush, brush egg onto piped dough; sprinkle with pearl sugar.
6. Bake, one pan at a time, for 10 minutes. Rotate pan, and bake until fully puffed and golden brown, about 10 minutes more. Let cool completely on pans. Best served same day as made. Store in an airtight container for up to 2 days.

White Cheddar-and-Chive Gougères

Makes about 18 pastries

Shifting to the savory side of choux, my gougères trade traditional Gruyère cheese for sharp white Cheddar, and delicate chives offer a hint of oniony flavor. Serve these puffs with your favorite wine—I love Chablis and even Champagne.

Choux Pastry Dough (recipe on page 136)
- **1 cup (114 grams) finely shredded sharp white Cheddar cheese, divided**
- **¼ cup (12 grams) plus 2 tablespoons (6 grams) finely chopped fresh chives, divided**

1. Preheat oven to 375°F (190°C). Line 2 to 3 baking sheets with parchment paper.
2. Using a permanent marker and a 2-inch round cutter as a guide, draw circles at least 1½ inches apart on another sheet of parchment paper; slide template under parchment on a prepared pan.
3. Prepare Choux Pastry Dough through step 2; add ½ cup (57 grams) cheese and ¼ cup (12 grams) chives, and beat at low speed until just combined.
4. Transfer batter to a large pastry bag fitted with a ½-inch round piping tip (Ateco #807). Place piping tip in center of a drawn circle. Holding tip perpendicularly ½ inch above parchment paper and stationary the entire time, apply even pressure until batter reaches edges of drawn circle. Stop applying pressure, and move tip in a quick circular motion as you lift away to help prevent a point from forming on top. Repeat with remaining batter until pan is full.
5. Wet your finger with water, and press down any points to create a smooth top, if necessary. Slide template out from under piped batter, and place under parchment on other prepared pans; pipe remaining batter.
6. Bake for 10 minutes. Rotate pans, and bake until fully puffed and deep golden brown, 10 to 15 minutes more. Sprinkle remaining ½ cup (57 grams) cheese and remaining 2 tablespoons (6 grams) chives onto hot pastries. Serve warm.

Cream Puffs

Makes about 30 pastries

Also called a profiterole, the cream puff is pâtisserie's crowning achievement of simplicity. Buttery, light-as-air dough bakes into fluffy rounds with a hollow center, begging to be filled with luscious crème mousseline. Dust with confectioners' sugar and pile them high; take joy in the uncomplicated perfection.

Choux Pastry Dough (recipe on page 136)
Vanilla Crème Mousseline (recipe follows)
Garnish: confectioners' sugar

1. Preheat oven to 375°F (190°C). Using a permanent marker and a 2-inch round cutter as a guide, draw 30 circles at least 2 inches apart on 2 to 3 sheets of parchment paper. Turn parchment over, and place on baking sheets.
2. Transfer Choux Pastry Dough to a large pastry bag fitted with a ½-inch round piping tip (Ateco #805). Place piping tip in center of a drawn circle. Holding tip perpendicularly ½ inch above parchment paper and stationary the entire time, apply even pressure until batter reaches edges of drawn circle. Stop applying pressure, and move tip in a quick circular motion as you lift away to help prevent a point from forming on top. Repeat with remaining batter until pan is full.
3. Wet your finger with water, and press down any points to create a smooth top, if necessary. Slide template out from under piped batter, and place under parchment on other prepared pans; pipe remaining batter.
4. Bake for 15 minutes. Rotate pans, and bake until fully puffed and deep golden brown, about 10 minutes more. Let cool completely on pans.
5. Using a ¼-inch round piping tip (Ateco #802), poke a hole in center of bottom of each puff. Insert a skewer into hole, and move it around to ensure cream will fill entire puff.
6. Transfer Vanilla Crème Mousseline to a large pastry bag fitted with same ¼-inch round piping tip. Place piping tip into hole, and gently fill. Repeat with remaining puffs and Vanilla Crème Mousseline. Refrigerate until ready to serve. Best served same day as made. Garnish with confectioners' sugar just before serving, if desired.

Vanilla Crème Mousseline

Makes about 5 cups

- **3 cups (720 grams) whole milk**
- **1 cup (200 grams) granulated sugar, divided**
- **1 vanilla bean, split lengthwise, seeds scraped and reserved**
- **8 large egg yolks (149 grams)**
- **¼ cup plus 3 tablespoons (56 grams) cornstarch**
- **¼ teaspoon kosher salt**
- **¼ cup (57 grams) unsalted butter, softened**
- **1½ cups (340 grams) unsalted butter, room temperature**

1. In a large saucepan, whisk together milk, ½ cup (100 grams) sugar, and vanilla bean and reserved seeds. Heat over medium heat until steaming. (Do not boil.) Discard vanilla bean.
2. In a large bowl, whisk together egg yolks, cornstarch, salt, and remaining ½ cup (100 grams) sugar. Gradually add warm milk mixture, whisking constantly. Pour egg yolk mixture into saucepan, and cook over medium heat, whisking constantly, until thickened and boiling, 4 to 5 minutes.
3. Strain mixture through a fine-mesh sieve into a large bowl. Stir in softened butter in two additions. Cover with plastic wrap, pressing wrap directly on surface of pastry cream to prevent a skin from forming. Refrigerate until an instant-read thermometer registers 65°F (18°C) to 70°F (21°C), 2½ to 3 hours.
4. In the bowl of a stand mixer fitted with the paddle attachment, beat room temperature butter at medium speed until smooth, about 1 minute.
5. Whisk refrigerated pastry cream until smooth. (At this point, butter and pastry cream should be same temperature.) With mixer on low speed, gradually add pastry cream to butter, beating until combined after each addition and stopping to scrape bottom and sides of bowl and paddle. Use immediately.

After baking and cooling, use a ¼-inch round piping tip to punch a small hole into the bottom of choux puff. Use a skewer to gently clean out the interior of lingering dough from hollow.

Pipe filling into bottom hole, being careful not to overfill so they do not burst.

Pâte à Choux:
CHOUX PASTRY DOUGH

Chocolate Éclairs

Makes 18 to 20 pastries

The term *éclair* translates literally to "flash of lightning," a reference to how quickly these oblong treats are eaten. Our version is a decadent chocolate affair, with a glossy glaze and silky cocoa cream filling.

Choux Pastry Dough (recipe on page 136)
Chocolate Crème Mousseline (recipe follows)
Chocolate Glaze (recipe follows)
Garnish: flaked sea salt

1. Preheat oven to 375°F (190°C). Using a marker and a ruler, draw 10 (4¼-inch) lines at least 2 inches apart onto 2 sheets of parchment paper. Turn parchment over, and place on baking sheets.
2. Transfer Choux Pastry Dough to pastry bag fitted with ½-inch French star piping tip (Ateco #867). Starting on lines farthest from you, start by applying even pressure. Then, hold tip about ¾ inch above parchment paper, and slowly pipe out oblong shapes. Begin to lessen pressure on pastry bag as you reach end of line; then, stop applying pressure, and lift up, leaving a small curl at end of éclair. Wet your finger with water, and press down tip on éclair. Repeat with remaining batter.
3. Bake, one pan at a time, for 10 minutes. Rotate pan, and bake until fully puffed and golden brown, 10 to 15 minutes more. Let cool completely on pans.
4. Using a ¼-inch round piping tip (Ateco #802), poke 2 holes about ¾ inch from each end on bottom of each éclair. Insert a skewer into holes, and move it around to ensure cream will fill entire éclair.
5. Transfer Chocolate Crème Mousseline to a large pastry bag fitted with same ¼-inch round piping tip. Place piping tip into one hole, and apply gentle pressure to begin filling éclair. Pipe mousseline into second hole until éclair feels heavy. Repeat with remaining éclairs and remaining mousseline.
6. Holding éclair by bottom half and parallel to surface of Chocolate Glaze, dip top of éclair in glaze. Still parallel, lift éclair out of glaze. Then, slowly lift one end of éclair, letting excess chocolate run off. Repeat with remaining éclairs. Garnish with sea salt, if desired. Refrigerate until ready to serve. Best served same day as made.

Chocolate Crème Mousseline

Makes about 6 cups

3 cups (720 grams) whole milk
1 cup (200 grams) granulated sugar, divided
1 vanilla bean, split lengthwise, seeds scraped and reserved
8 large egg yolks (149 grams)
¼ cup plus 3 tablespoons (56 grams) cornstarch
¼ teaspoon kosher salt
¼ cup (57 grams) unsalted butter, softened
1½ cups (255 grams) bittersweet chocolate, melted and slightly cooled
1½ cups (340 grams) unsalted butter, room temperature

1. In a large saucepan, whisk together milk, ½ cup (100 grams) sugar, and vanilla bean and reserved seeds. Heat over medium heat until steaming. (Do not boil.) Discard vanilla bean.
2. In a large bowl, whisk together egg yolks, cornstarch, salt, and remaining ½ cup (100 grams) sugar. Gradually add to egg mixture, whisking constantly. Pour egg mixture into saucepan, and cook over medium heat, whisking constantly, until thickened and boiling, 4 to 5 minutes.
3. Strain mixture through a fine-mesh sieve into a large bowl. Stir in softened butter in two additions. Fold in melted chocolate. Cover with plastic wrap, pressing wrap directly on surface of pastry cream to prevent a skin from forming. Refrigerate until an instant-read thermometer registers 65°F (18°C) to 70°F (21°C), 2½ to 3 hours.
4. In the bowl of a stand mixer fitted with the paddle attachment, beat room temperature butter at medium speed until smooth, about 1 minute.
5. Whisk refrigerated pastry cream until smooth. (At this point, butter and pastry cream should be same temperature.) With mixer on low speed, gradually add pastry cream to butter, beating until combined after each addition and stopping to scrape bottom and sides of bowl and paddle. Use immediately.

Chocolate Glaze

Makes about 2 cups

- **8 ounces (225 grams) 60% cacao bittersweet chocolate, chopped**
- **1 cup plus 2 tablespoons (270 grams) heavy whipping cream**
- **1 tablespoon plus 1 teaspoon (28 grams) light corn syrup**
- **¼ teaspoon kosher salt**
- **2 tablespoons (28 grams) unsalted butter, softened**

1. Place chocolate in a medium heatproof bowl.
2. In a small saucepan, heat cream, corn syrup, and salt over medium heat until steaming. (Do not boil.) Pour hot cream mixture onto chocolate. Let stand for 30 seconds; whisk until melted. Whisk in butter until melted and mixture is smooth. Use immediately.

Use a ¼-inch piping tip to punch 2 holes about ¾ inch from each end on bottom of each éclair. Fill with Chocolate Crème Mousseline.

Holding éclair by bottom half and parallel to surface of Chocolate Glaze, dip top of éclair in glaze. Lift éclair straight up out of glaze, then lift one end of éclair and let excess run off.

Lemon Meringue Éclairs

Makes about 14 pastries

Each bite of this éclair is a balance of crisp choux pastry, creamy lemon filling, and lightly toasted meringue.

Choux Pastry Dough (recipe on page 136)
Lemon Curd (recipe follows)
Swiss Meringue (recipe follows)

1. Preheat oven to 375°F (190°C). Using a marker and a ruler, draw 10 (4¼-inch) lines at least 2 inches apart on 2 sheets of parchment paper. Turn parchment over, and place on baking sheets.
2. Transfer Choux Pastry Dough to a pastry bag fitted with ½-inch French star piping tip (Ateco #867). Starting on lines farthest from you, start by applying even pressure. Then, hold tip about ¾ inch above parchment paper, and slowly pipe out oblong shapes. Begin to lessen pressure on pastry bag as you reach end of line; then, stop applying pressure, and lift up, leaving a small curl at end of éclair. Wet your finger with water, and press down tip on éclair. Repeat with remaining batter.
3. Bake, one pan at a time, for 10 minutes. Rotate pan, and bake until fully puffed and deep golden brown, 10 to 15 minutes more. Let cool completely on pans.
4. Using a ¼-inch round piping tip (Ateco #802) , poke 2 holes about ¾ inch from each end on bottom of each éclair. Insert a skewer into holes, and move it around to ensure curd will fill entire éclair.
5. Transfer Lemon Curd to a large pastry bag fitted with same ¼-inch round piping tip. Place piping tip into one hole, and apply gentle pressure to begin filling éclair. Pipe curd into second hole until éclair feels heavy. Repeat with remaining éclairs and remaining curd.
6. Spoon Swiss Meringue into a pastry bag fitted with a ½-inch star piping tip (Ateco #864). Pipe swirls onto éclairs. Using a handheld kitchen torch, carefully brown meringue. Refrigerate until ready to serve. Best served same day as made.

Lemon Curd

Makes 1¼ cups

- ⅓ **cup plus 1 tablespoon (79 grams) granulated sugar**
- 2 **large eggs (100 grams), room temperature**
- 2 **teaspoons (4 grams) packed lemon zest**
- 1 **teaspoon (3 grams) cornstarch**
- ¼ **teaspoon kosher salt**
- ½ **cup (120 grams) fresh lemon juice**
- ⅓ **cup (76 grams) unsalted butter, cubed**

1. In a medium saucepan, whisk together sugar, eggs, lemon zest, cornstarch, and salt until smooth. Whisk in lemon juice until smooth. Cook over medium-low heat, whisking constantly, until mixture is thick, bubbly, and registers 170°F (76°C) on an instant-read thermometer, about 7 minutes.
2. Strain mixture through a fine-mesh sieve into a medium heatproof bowl. Whisk in butter, one cube at a time, until melted and smooth after each addition. Cover with plastic wrap, pressing wrap directly on surface of curd to prevent a skin from forming. Let cool completely before using. Refrigerate in an airtight container for up to 1 week.

Swiss Meringue

Makes 1¼ cups

- ½ **cup (100 grams) extra-fine granulated sugar or castor sugar**
- ¼ **cup (60 grams) egg whites, room temperature**
- ¼ **teaspoon cream of tartar**
- ⅛ **teaspoon kosher salt**
- ¼ **teaspoon (1 gram) vanilla extract**

1. In the heatproof bowl of a stand mixer, whisk together sugar, egg whites, cream of tartar, and salt. Place bowl over a saucepan of simmering water, and cook, whisking frequently, until sugar completely dissolves and an instant-read thermometer registers 120°F (49°C) to 130°F (54°C).
2. Carefully return bowl to stand mixer. Using the whisk attachment, beat at high speed until stiff peaks form and bowl is cool to the touch, 4 to 5 minutes. Beat in vanilla. Use immediately.

Pâte à Choux:
CHOUX PASTRY DOUGH

Hazelnut Paris-Brests

Makes 12 to 14 pastries

Invented to commemorate a famous bicycle race that ran from Paris to Brest, the Paris-Brest is choux piped in a circle to resemble a bicycle tire and is covered in toasted nuts and filled with a rich nut cream. I chose a velvety hazelnut mousse and a crunchy hazelnut-studded caramel glaze.

Choux Pastry Dough (recipe on page 136)
Caramel (recipe follows)
Candied Hazelnuts (recipe follows)
Praline Crème Mousseline (recipe follows)

1. Preheat oven to 375°F (190°C). Using a marker and a 3-inch round cutter as a guide, draw 14 circles at least 2 inches apart on 2 to 3 sheets of parchment paper. Turn parchment over, and place on baking sheets.
2. Transfer Choux Pastry Dough to pastry bag fitted with ½-inch French star piping tip (Ateco #867). Place tip on a drawn circle, and start by applying even pressure. Then, hold tip about ¾ inch above parchment paper, and slowly pipe around drawn circle. Begin to lessen pressure on pastry bag as you come to end of circle; then, stop applying pressure, letting it overlap slightly. Wet your finger with water, and smooth down overlap. Repeat with remaining batter.
3. Bake for 15 minutes. Rotate pans, and bake until puffed and golden brown, about 10 minutes more. Let cool completely on pans.
4. Place a sheet of parchment paper on work surface. Holding pastry by bottom half and parallel to surface of Caramel, carefully dip top of pastry in Caramel. Still parallel, lift pastry out of Caramel, letting excess drip off. Gently place on prepared parchment. Immediately sprinkle with Candied Hazelnuts. Repeat with remaining pastries.
5. Using a serrated knife, cut each pastry in half horizontally. Transfer Praline Crème Mousseline to a pastry bag fitted with a ⅜-inch open star piping tip (Ateco #824). Pipe tall rosettes on bottom half of each pastry. Cover with top half of each pastry, and gently press down. Refrigerate until ready to serve. Best served same day as made.

Caramel

Makes about 2 cups

3 cups (600 grams) granulated sugar
¾ cup (180 grams) water, plus more for brushing

1. In a medium saucepan, stir together sugar and ¾ cup (180 grams) water until moistened. (It should look like wet sand.) Heat over medium heat. Using a pastry brush, brush sides of pan with water. Stir gently while sugar is dissolving. Increase heat to high. Do not stir after sugar mixture starts to boil. Cook until mixture is amber colored. Remove from heat, and immediately plunge pan into an ice water bath for 5 seconds to stop the cooking process. Let cool for 5 minutes before using.

Candied Hazelnuts

Makes about 4½ cups

2⅔ cups (379 grams) skinned whole hazelnuts
1½ cups (300 grams) granulated sugar
4½ tablespoons (68 grams) water, plus more for brushing
1½ teaspoons (5 grams) flaked sea salt

1. Preheat oven to 300°F (150°C).
2. On a rimmed baking sheet, spread hazelnuts in an even layer.
3. Bake until fragrant and lightly browned, about 15 minutes. Let cool completely. Chop hazelnuts. Line same rimmed baking sheet with a nonstick baking mat.
4. In a medium saucepan, stir together sugar and 4½ tablespoons (68 grams) water until moistened. (It should look like wet sand.) Heat over high heat. Using a pastry brush, brush down sides of pan with water. Stir gently while sugar is dissolving. Do not stir after sugar mixture starts to boil. Cook until mixture is light amber colored. Remove from heat, and quickly stir in chopped hazelnuts. Pour onto prepared pan. Using a heatproof spatula, spread candied hazelnuts in a single layer, and sprinkle with salt. Let cool completely.
5. Gently tap candied hazelnuts on baking sheet to break into smaller pieces. Using a chef's knife, chop into small pieces. Reserve 1¾ cups (225 grams) for Praline Crème Mousseline; store remainder in an airtight contianer for up to 5 days.

Hold tip about ¾ inch above parchment paper, and slowly pipe around drawn circle. Begin to lessen pressure on pastry bag as you come to end of circle; then, stop applying pressure, letting it overlap slightly. Wet your finger with water, and smooth down overlap.

Pipe mousseline in tall rosettes onto bottom half of each pastry.

Praline Crème Mousseline

Makes about 6 cups

- 3 cups (720 grams) whole milk
- 1 cup (200 grams) granulated sugar, divided
- 1 vanilla bean, split lengthwise, seeds scraped and reserved
- 8 large egg yolks (149 grams)
- ¼ cup plus 3 tablespoons (56 grams) cornstarch
- ¼ teaspoon kosher salt
- ¼ cup (57 grams) unsalted butter, softened
- 1¾ cups (225 grams) Candied Hazelnuts (recipe precedes)
- 1½ cups (340 grams) unsalted butter, room temperature

1. In a large saucepan, heat milk, ½ cup (100 grams) sugar, and vanilla bean and reserved seeds over medium heat until steaming, whisking occasionally. (Do not boil.) Discard vanilla bean.

2. In a large bowl, whisk together egg yolks, cornstarch, salt, and remaining ½ cup (100 grams) sugar. Gradually add warm milk mixture, whisking constantly. Pour egg mixture into saucepan; cook over medium heat, whisking constantly, until thickened and bubbly, 4 to 5 minutes.

3. Strain mixture through a fine-mesh sieve into a large bowl. Stir in softened butter in two additions. Cover with plastic wrap, pressing directly on surface of pastry cream to prevent a skin from forming. Refrigerate until an instant-read thermometer registers 65°F (18°C) to 70°F (21°C), 2½ to 3 hours.

4. In the work bowl of a food processor, process Candied Hazelnuts until a paste forms, about 2 minutes.

5. In the bowl of a stand mixer fitted with the paddle attachment, beat room temperature butter at medium speed until smooth, about 1 minute.

6. Whisk refrigerated pastry cream until smooth. (At this point, butter and pastry cream should be same temperature.) With mixer on low speed, gradually add pastry cream to butter, beating until combined after each addition and stopping to scrape bottom and sides of bowl and paddle. Refrigerate, stirring every 15 minutes, until thickend and pipable, about 1 hour.

Chocolate-Glazed Mini Croquembouches

Makes 3 small pastry trees/85 to 95 pastries

My simplified version of classic croquembouche is designed to bring you all the showstopping glamour of the original but with just half the trouble. I kept the traditional golden choux dough and luxuriously silky pastry cream, but I traded the complex sugar work for a simple chocolate glaze, gluing the cream puffs together with a cocoa drizzle rather than hot spun sugar. The result is a trio of glittering croquembouche pyramids ready to adorn any special-occasion table.

Choux Pastry Dough (recipe on page 136)
Vanilla Pastry Cream (recipe follows)

Glaze:

- 3 **ounces (85 grams) unsweetened chocolate, finely chopped (about ½ cup)**
- 6 **tablespoons (84 grams) refined coconut oil**
- 1½ **teaspoons (9 grams) vanilla bean paste**
- 3 **cups (360 grams) confectioners' sugar, sifted**
- 7 **tablespoons (105 grams) warm whole milk (105°F/41°C to 110°F/43°C)**

Garnish: assorted gold sprinkles

1. Preheat oven to 375°F (190°C). Line baking sheets with parchment paper.
2. Using a permanent marker, draw 24 (1¼-inch) circles 2 inches apart on a sheet of parchment paper. Slide template under parchment on a prepared pan.
3. Place piping tip in center of a drawn circle. Holding tip perpendicularly ½ inch above parchment paper and stationary the entire time, apply even pressure until batter reaches edges of drawn circle. Stop applying pressure, and move tip in a quick circular motion as you lift away to help prevent a point from forming on top. Repeat with remaining batter until pan is full.
4. Wet your finger with water, and press down any points to create a smooth top, if necessary. Slide template out from under piped batter, and place under parchment on other prepared pans; pipe remaining batter.
5. Bake, one pan at a time, for 10 minutes. Rotate pan, and bake until fully puffed and golden brown, 10 to 15 minutes more. Let cool completely on pans.
6. Using a ¼-inch round piping tip (Ateco #802), poke a hole in center of bottom of each puff. Insert a skewer into hole, and move it around to ensure pastry cream will fill entire puff.
7. Transfer Vanilla Pastry Cream to a large pastry bag fitted with same ¼-inch round piping tip. Place piping tip into hole, and gently fill. Repeat with remaining puffs and remaining Vanilla Pastry Cream. Refrigerate for up to 1 hour.
8. For glaze: In a small saucepan, heat chocolate and coconut oil over medium-low heat, stirring frequently, until melted and well combined. Remove from heat. Stir in vanilla bean paste. Gradually add confectioners' sugar alternately with warm milk, beginning and ending with confectioners' sugar, whisking until combined after each addition. Whisk until smooth and combined. (Mixture will be shiny and thickened; it will fall off a whisk in ribbons and be the consistency of hot fudge sauce.) Transfer glaze to a medium heatproof bowl.
9. To build one "tree," arrange 12 puffs in a filled circle in a single layer on desired serving plate. Using a spoon, drizzle glaze onto puffs, spreading as desired. Arrange 8 puffs on top of first layer; drizzle glaze onto puffs, spreading as desired. Arrange 5 puffs on top of previous layer; drizzle glaze onto puffs, spreading as desired. Repeat procedure in layers of 3 and 1. Garnish with sprinkles, if desired. Repeat procedure with remaining puffs to build 2 more "trees." Serve immediately. Best eaten same day as made.

Vanilla Pastry Cream

Makes about 5¼ cups

- 5 **cups (1,200 grams) whole milk, divided**
- 1 **cup (200 grams) granulated sugar, divided**

- 7 tablespoons (56 grams) cornstarch
- ¼ cup (31 grams) all-purpose flour
- 1 teaspoon (3 grams) kosher salt
- 7 large egg yolks (130 grams)
- 7 tablespoons (98 grams) unsalted butter, softened
- 1½ tablespoons (27 grams) vanilla bean paste

1. In a medium saucepan, heat 4 cups (960 grams) milk and ½ cup (100 grams) sugar over medium heat, whisking occasionally, just until steaming. (Do not boil.)
2. In a medium bowl, whisk together cornstarch, flour, salt, and remaining ½ cup (100 grams) sugar. Whisk in egg yolks and remaining 1 cup (240 grams) milk until well combined. Gradually add half of warm milk mixture to egg yolk mixture, whisking constantly. Add egg yolk mixture to remaining warm milk mixture in pan. Bring to a boil over medium heat, whisking constantly. Cook, whisking constantly, until thickened and bubbly, about 2 minutes.
3. Remove from heat. Whisk in butter until melted and smooth. Strain through a fine-mesh sieve into a shallow heatproof dish. Whisk in vanilla bean paste. Cover with plastic wrap, pressing wrap directly on surface of pastry cream to prevent a skin from forming. Refrigerate until thick and cold, at least 4 hours or up to overnight. Just before using, whisk pastry cream until smooth.

Assembling the Croquembouche

To build one "tree," arrange 12 puffs in a filled circle in a single layer on serving plate. Drizzle glaze onto puffs, spreading as desired. Arrange 8 puff on top of first layer, and drizzle with glaze, spreading as desired.

TIP: Stir the glaze periodically; if needed, microwave on high in 5-second intervals until loosened.

Repeat process in layers of 5, 3, and 1. Garnish with sprinkles, if desired. Repeat procedure with remaining puffs to build 2 more "trees."

TIP: Since puff yields may vary slightly, it's a good idea to count them beforehand and divvy out the amount for each tree, adjusting layers as needed. Any extras can (and should) be enjoyed as snacks!

Pâte à Choux:
CHOUX PASTRY DOUGH

French Crullers with Citrus Glaze

Makes 9 to 10 doughnuts

For decadent doughnuts, I pipe choux pastry dough into rounds, fry them until golden brown, and dip them in a bright and tangy lemon and orange glaze.

1 cup plus 2 tablespoons (141 grams) all-purpose flour
½ teaspoon (1 gram) ground cardamom
¼ teaspoon ground ginger
1 cup (240 grams) water
6 tablespoons (84 grams) unsalted butter, cubed and softened
1 tablespoon (12 grams) granulated sugar
½ teaspoon (1.5 grams) kosher salt
½ teaspoon (2 grams) vanilla extract
3 large eggs (150 grams), room temperature
1 large egg white (30 grams), room temperature
Vegetable oil, for frying
Citrus Glaze (recipe follows)

1. Spray a large rimmed baking sheet with cooking spray. Cut 10 (3¼-inch) square pieces of parchment paper; place on prepared pan. Spray parchment with cooking spray.
2. In a small bowl, whisk together flour, cardamom, and ginger.
3. In a medium saucepan, bring 1 cup (240 grams) water, butter, sugar, salt, and vanilla to a boil over medium-high heat, stirring occasionally. Remove from heat; add flour mixture, stirring with a wooden spoon until combined. Return mixture to medium-high heat; cook, stirring constantly, until mixture is smooth and a skin forms on bottom of pan, about 2 minutes.
4. Transfer mixture to the bowl of a stand mixer fitted with the paddle attachment, and beat at medium-low speed for 2 minutes. Add eggs, one at a time, beating until combined after each addition and stopping to scrape sides of bowl. (Batter will appear broken but will come back together as eggs are incorporated.) Add egg white; beat until a smooth, glossy dough forms. (Dough should fall off the paddle attachment in the shape of a "V" and will hold a slight peak when pinched between fingers.) Cover and refrigerate for 30 minutes.
5. Transfer dough to a pastry bag fitted with a ½-inch open star piping tip (Ateco #827). Applying even pressure, pipe a large circle within each prepared parchment square. To join ends, gently press piping tip into starting point of circle; release pressure and then pull up while continuing to trace around circle. (Dough will pinch off.) Wet your finger with water; gently smooth and seal overlapping ends. Let stand at room temperature for 20 minutes.
6. In a large heavy-bottomed saucepan or Dutch oven, pour oil to a depth of 2 inches, and heat over medium heat until a deep-fry thermometer registers 370°F (188°C).
7. Line a baking sheet with parchment paper; place a wire rack on prepared pan.
8. Working in batches, carefully add piped dough to oil, parchment side up. Cook until puffed and golden brown, about 3 minutes per side, discarding parchment halfway through frying. (It's OK if some crullers burst slightly in spots.) Using a spider strainer or large slotted spoon, remove crullers, and let drain on prepared rack. Let cool for about 15 minutes.
9. Working one at a time, gently dip cruller in Citrus Glaze, using a fork to turn to fully coat. Using 2 forks, gently lift out of glaze, letting excess drip off, and return to rack. Let stand until glaze is set, about 15 minutes. Best served same day as made.

Citrus Glaze

Makes about 1⅓ cups

3 cups (360 grams) confectioners' sugar, sifted
5 tablespoons (75 grams) whole milk
2½ tablespoons (52.5 grams) light corn syrup
2 teaspoons (4 grams) packed lemon zest
1 teaspoon (5 grams) tightly packed orange zest
½ teaspoon (1.5 grams) kosher salt
½ teaspoons (2 grams) vanilla extract

1. In a medium bowl, whisk together all ingredients until smooth. Use immediately.

Applying even pressure, pipe a large circle within each prepared parchment square. To join ends, gently press piping tip into starting point of circle; release pressure and then pull up while continuing to trace around circle. Dough will naturally pinch off, so don't panic.

Wet your finger with water; gently smooth and seal overlapping ends. Don't fuss over making it look perfect. When you fry your crullers, slight cracks and some burst bubbles are bound to happen—they will still be delicious.

TIP: This is a deflated cruller that has been fried for too short of a time. If you take it out too quickly, the choux will deflate rapidly once out of the oil. Keep your eye on the temperature and the timer when frying.

Pâte à Choux:
CHOUX PASTRY DOUGH

Cinnamon Sugar Churros

Makes about 24 churros

Churros have wonderfully crisp ridges on the outside yet are delicate and buttery on the inside. These Mexican-inspired churros are tossed in cinnamon sugar and dunked in dark chocolate sauce subtly spiced with red pepper and cinnamon, which are characteristic spices found in Mexican hot chocolate. These light, crunchy pastries rise beautifully not from yeast or a chemical leavening agent but because they're made with pâte à choux!

---

1 cup (240 grams) water
6 tablespoons (84 grams) unsalted butter, cubed and softened
¾ cup (150 grams) plus 1 tablespoon (12 grams) granulated sugar, divided
½ teaspoon (1.5 grams) kosher salt
½ teaspoon (2 grams) vanilla extract
1 cup plus 2 tablespoons (141 grams) all-purpose flour
3 large eggs (150 grams), room temperature
1 large egg white (30 grams), room temperature
Vegetable oil, for frying
1½ teaspoons (3 grams) ground cinnamon
Cinnamon Chocolate Sauce (recipe follows)

1. In a medium saucepan, bring 1 cup (240 grams) water, butter, 1 tablespoon (12 grams) sugar, salt, and vanilla to a boil over medium-high heat, stirring occasionally. Remove from heat; add flour, stirring with a wooden spoon until combined. Return mixture to medium-high heat; cook, stirring constantly, until mixture is smooth and a skin forms on bottom of pan, about 2 minutes.
2. Transfer mixture to the bowl of a stand mixer fitted with the paddle attachment, and beat at low speed until cooled slightly, about 1 minute. Add eggs, one at a time, beating until combined after each addition and stopping to scrape sides of bowl. (Batter will appear broken but will come back together as eggs are incorporated.) Add egg white; beat until a smooth, glossy dough forms. (Dough should fall off the paddle attachment in the shape of a "V" and will hold a slight peak when pinched between fingers.) Cover and refrigerate for 30 minutes.
3. In a large heavy-bottomed saucepan or Dutch oven, pour oil to a depth of 2 inches, and heat over medium heat until a deep-fry thermometer registers 360°F (182°C) to 365°F (185°C).
4. Line a rimmed baking sheet with paper towels.
5. In a shallow dish, whisk together cinnamon and remaining ¾ cup (150 grams) sugar.
6. Transfer dough to pastry bag fitted with a ⅜-inch closed star piping tip (Ateco #844). Carefully pipe dough in batches (2 or 3 at a time) in a straight line about 6 inches in length into hot oil. Using kitchen shears, cut dough at end closest to piping tip when it gets to desired length. (If dough is not staying straight in oil, use tongs to help straighten dough immediately after piping, if desired.)
7. Fry until puffed and golden brown, 1½ to 2 minutes per side. Remove from oil using tongs or a large slotted spoon, and let drain on prepared pan. Dredge hot churros in cinnamon sugar. Serve warm with Cinnamon Chocolate Sauce.

Cinnamon Chocolate Sauce

Makes about 1 cup

⅓ cup (80 grams) heavy whipping cream, plus more if desired
½ cup (100 grams) granulated sugar
¼ cup (57 grams) unsalted butter
⅓ cup (25 grams) unsweetened cocoa powder, sifted
3 tablespoons (63 grams) light corn syrup
½ teaspoon (1 gram) ground cinnamon
¼ teaspoon kosher salt
⅛ teaspoon ground red pepper (optional)
0.5 ounce (14 grams) unsweetened chocolate, chopped

1. In a medium saucepan, heat cream, sugar, and butter over medium-low heat, whisking frequently, until butter is melted and sugar dissolves. Whisk in cocoa, corn syrup, cinnamon, salt, and red pepper (if using); cook, whisking constantly, until smooth and well combined, 2 to 3 minutes. Whisk in chocolate until melted. Serve warm. (If a thinner consistency is desired, remove from heat, and whisk in cream 1 teaspoon at a time.) Refrigerate in an airtight container for up to 1 week.

pâte battue and pâte tournée

cake batter and cookie dough

MACARONS, MADELEINES, GÂTEAU OPÉRA

Pâte battue, or "beaten dough," and *pâte tournée*, "turned dough," are used to create numerous classic French cakes and cookies. These batters and doughs are traditionally leavened by beating or whipping in air to achieve a soft and light texture.

Chocolate Hazelnut Macarons

Makes about 36 macarons

Like so many other pastries, this classic cookie is comprised of simple ingredients, but the magic occurs in the method of combining the elements to yield an exquisite payoff.

1½ cups (144 grams) superfine blanched almond flour
1¼ cups (150 grams) confectioners' sugar
1 tablespoon (5 grams) Dutch process cocoa powder
4 large egg whites (120 grams), room temperature and divided
¾ cup (150 grams) granulated sugar
¼ cup (60 grams) water
¼ teaspoon cream of tartar
Finely chopped hazelnuts, for sprinkling
Hazelnut-Chocolate Ganache (recipe follows)

1. Line rimmed baking sheets with silicone baking mats.
2. In the work bowl of a food processor, pulse flour, confectioners' sugar, and cocoa until finely ground and well combined. Sift mixture through a large fine-mesh sieve into a large bowl, discarding any solids. Add 2 egg whites (60 grams); fold until combined. Cover with plastic wrap to prevent drying out.
3. In a small saucepan, stir together granulated sugar and ¼ cup (60 grams) water. Cook over high heat, without stirring, until an instant-read thermometer registers 240°F (116°C) to 245°F (118°C).
4. Meanwhile, in the bowl of a stand mixer fitted with the whisk attachment, beat cream of tartar and remaining 2 egg whites (60 grams) at low speed until foamy. Increase mixer speed to medium-high, and beat until medium-stiff peaks form. (Egg whites and sugar syrup should be prepared so they are ready at the same time.)
5. With mixer on high speed, add sugar syrup to whipped egg white mixture, carefully pouring straight into mixture, avoiding whisk attachment and side of bowl. Beat until mixture is cooled and stiff peaks form, about 4 minutes.
6. Add one-fourth of meringue (about ½ cup or 60 grams) to flour mixture; stir vigorously until combined. Add remaining meringue, and carefully fold until mixture is ribbon-consistency. (Mixture should be thick and slowly but freely fall off the spatula in a "V" shape; when you drag the spatula through the batter, it should move like lava and slowly come back together.)
7. Transfer batter to a pastry bag fitted with a medium round piping tip (Ateco #804). Holding pastry bag with opening of tip perpendicular to a prepared pan, pipe batter within circles on baking mats, applying pressure and leaving tip stationary until batter just reaches edge of circle. Move and lift piping tip in a quick circular motion as you finish piping each macaron shell to prevent a point from forming on top. Vigorously slam pans on counter 5 to 7 times to release air bubbles. Sprinkle with hazelnuts. Let stand at room temperature until a skin forms on top of macaron shells, 30 minutes to 1 hour. (Batter should be matte, feel dry to the touch, and should not stick to your finger.)
8. Preheat oven to 300°F (150°C).
9. Bake, one pan at a time, until shells are firm but have a slight wobble to the touch, 13 to 15 minutes. Let cool completely on pan on a wire rack.
10. Spoon Hazelnut-Chocolate Ganache into a pastry bag fitted with a medium round piping tip (Ateco #804). Pipe ganache onto flat side of half of macaron shells. Lightly press remaining macaron shells, flat side down, on top of ganache. Refrigerate in an airtight container for up to 3 days.

Hazelnut-Chocolate Ganache

Makes about 1 cup

½ cup (132 grams) hazelnut-chocolate spread
5 tablespoons (75 grams) heavy whipping cream
2 tablespoons (28 grams) unsalted butter
¼ teaspoon kosher salt

1. In a medium microwave-safe bowl, heat all ingredients on high in 30-second intervals, stirring between each, until butter is melted and mixture is smooth and well combined. Cover and let cool to room temperature. Use immediately.

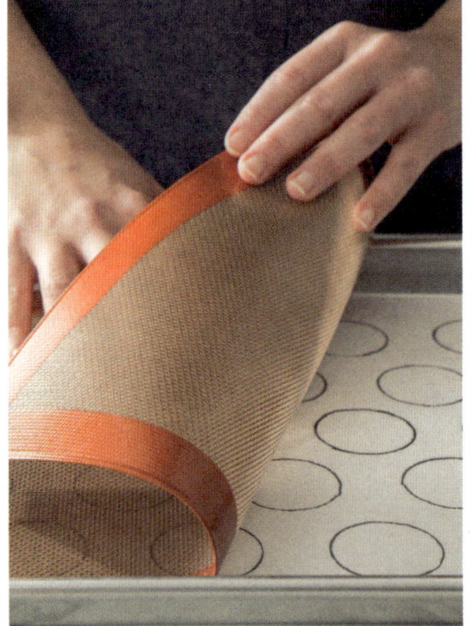

Macaron Method

Line rimmed baking sheets with silicone baking mats. Use a permanent marker to draw 1½-inch circles about 1 inch apart on a piece of parchment paper. Place template under a baking mat.
TIP: I use silicone baking mats instead of parchment paper because the macaron shells can stick to parchment and not rise properly in the oven. Mats also allow for a clean release. Meanwhile, the template helps you keep your piping consistent and ensures each macaron shell is the same size.

In the work bowl of a food processor, pulse flour, confectioners' sugar, and cocoa until finely ground and well combined. Sift mixture through a large fine-mesh sieve into a large bowl, discarding any solids.
TIP: The food processor will help remove any lumps and aerate the dry ingredients before you fold them into the egg white mixture. Specifically, the food processor speeds up the process, so you don't have to sift the dry ingredients three times. However, if you don't have a food processor, sifting three times will create the same results.

Peek at Your Peak

How do you know when your meringue is ready? You can overwhip your whites, which has negative effects on the cookies. Whites should be shiny and smooth, not grainy or dry. To know when you have proper stiff peaks, lift the whisk out and check to see if the peak has a slight bend. You can also turn the bowl upside down, and if the meringue stays steadily in place and doesn't fall out, you'll know it's ready. If your meringue starts to look clotted or textured, you have overwhipped it and should start the process over. Now that you've whipped it, use it immediately. Your meringue will begin to deflate and separate with every minute you wait.

Perfecting Piping

Transfer batter to a piping bag fitted with a medium round tip (Ateco #804). Using a medium tip is important because if it is too big, it will not help push air out while the batter is being piped, leaving air bubbles in the batter. For a mess-free batter transfer, place pastry bag in a large jar or glass and fold the bag edges over the lip of the glass before spooning in batter.

Holding tip perpendicular to pan, pipe batter onto drawn circles of template underneath mat. Apply pressure to bag, leaving tip stationary, until batter reaches drawn circle. If you move around while piping, the top won't be smooth. Release pressure, and move piping tip in a quick circular motion as you finish piping each macaron shell to prevent a tip from forming on top. Remove template, and place under second baking mat to pipe batter. Repeat procedure with remaining batter. Slam pans vigorously on counter 5 to 7 times, rotating pan 180 degrees each time, to release air bubbles.

Let stand at room temperature until a skin forms on top of macaron shells, anywhere from 30 minutes to 1 hour. (The batter should be matte, feel dry to the touch, and should not stick to your finger.) The time will depend on the environment in which it's resting. For example, if it's humid, it will take longer for the batter to set up. This wait time gives the cookies their signature crunchy shell and will help them develop a "foot."

Foot Check

The "foot" of a macaron is the iconic indicator of a well-made and well-baked macaron. Resembling a frill or ruffle at the base of the shell, the foot should be pronounced but unbroken. If your foot is nonexistent, you might have overwhipped or underwhipped your meringue, and the oven temperature might not have been high enough to get the macarons to rise quickly. If the foot has spread out too much into a frothy-looking barrier, the oven temperature might have been too high, forcing the shells to spread instead of rise. It will take some understanding of your oven (I recommend having an oven thermometer for accurate temperature readings) and meringue to get that ideal foot.

Five-Spice Madeleines

Makes 18 madeleines

These cake-like treats are named after their alleged creator, Madeleine. Lightly crisp on the outside and pillowy inside, the shell shape is a defining feature of these classic beauties. Cover in a mix of sugar and five-spice powder for a bite of subtle warmth.

½ cup (113 grams) unsalted butter, melted and divided, plus more for brushing pan
⅓ cup (67 grams) plus ¼ cup (50 grams) granulated sugar, divided
1 large egg (50 grams), room temperature
1 tablespoon (18 grams) vanilla bean paste
1 tablespoon (21 grams) honey
½ cup plus 2 tablespoons (79 grams) all-purpose flour
2 teaspoons (6 grams) orange zest
½ teaspoon plus ⅛ teaspoon (3 grams) baking powder
¼ teaspoon kosher salt
½ teaspoon (1 gram) Chinese five-spice powder

1. Preheat oven to 400°F (200°C). Brush wells of 2 madeleine pans with melted butter, and spray with baking spray with flour.
2. In the bowl of a stand mixer fitted with the paddle attachment, beat ⅓ cup (67 grams) sugar, egg, vanilla bean paste, and honey at high speed until pale yellow and thick, about 4 minutes.
3. In a small bowl, whisk together flour, orange zest, baking powder, and salt. With mixer on medium-low speed, gradually add flour mixture to sugar mixture, beating until just combined. Slowly add ¼ cup (56.5 grams) melted butter, beating until combined, about 1 minute. Using a 1-tablespoon spring-loaded scoop, scoop 1 tablespoon (14 grams) batter into each prepared well. (Place batter in deep end of each well, not center. Do not smooth or flatten.) Freeze for 7 minutes.
4. Bake until edges are golden and centers are puffed, 4 to 6 minutes. Let cool in pans for 1 minute. Remove from pans, and let cool completely on wire racks.
5. In another small bowl, combine five-spice powder and remaining ¼ cup (50 grams) sugar. Lightly brush madeleines with remaining ¼ cup (56.5 grams) melted butter, and dredge in sugar mixture. Best served same day as day. Store in an airtight container for up to 3 days.

Hazelnut Financiers

Makes 16 financiers

Financiers are always an elegant affair, but baked into fluted barquette molds, they take on a new dimension of refinement. I sweetened these with a touch of honey, but the real showstopper is the literal crowning glory: crunchy, salty candied nuts.

½ cup plus 4 tablespoons (169 grams) unsalted butter, softened and divided
2 tablespoons (42 grams) honey
1½ cups (140 grams) hazelnut flour
¾ cup plus 2 tablespoons (174 grams) granulated sugar
½ cup (60 grams) all-purpose flour
¼ teaspoon kosher salt
3 large egg whites (90 grams), room temperature
1 tablespoon (18 grams) vanilla bean paste
Candied Hazelnuts (recipe follows)

1. Preheat oven to 400°F (200°C). Using 2 tablespoons (28 grams) butter, heavily butter 16 (5-inch) barquette molds or a 24-cup mini muffin pan. Place molds on a baking sheet, and freeze until ready to use.
2. In a medium saucepan, melt remaining ½ cup plus 2 tablespoons (141 grams) butter over medium heat. Cook until butter turns a medium-brown color and has a nutty aroma, about 10 minutes. Remove from heat; stir in honey. Let cool slightly.
3. In a large bowl, whisk together hazelnut flour, sugar, all-purpose flour, and salt. Add egg whites and vanilla bean paste, whisking until smooth. Slowly whisk in browned butter mixture just until incorporated. Spoon batter into prepared molds or muffin cups, filling three-fourths full. Tap molds to level batter. (See Note.) With molds still on baking sheet, place in oven.
4. Immediately reduce oven temperature to 375°F (190°C). Bake until a wooden pick inserted in center comes out clean, about 15 minutes, rotating pan halfway through baking. (Alternatively, bake in mini muffin pan for 13 to 14 minutes.) Let cool completely in molds or muffin pan on wire racks.
5. Unmold financiers, using a knife if needed. Just before serving, top with Candied Hazelnuts. Best served same day as made. Store plain financiers in an airtight container for up to 1 week; top with Candied Hazelnuts just before serving.

Note: *If you do not have 16 molds and need to bake in batches, keep the batter refrigerated. Do not stir remaining batter.*

Candied Hazelnuts

Makes about 1 cup

½ cup (100 grams) granulated sugar
1½ tablespoons (22.5 grams) water
½ cup (71 grams) dry-roasted hazelnuts, halved
½ teaspoon (1.5 grams) flaked sea salt

1. Line a baking sheet with a nonstick baking mat.
2. In a small saucepan, stir together sugar and 1½ tablespoons (22.5 grams) water just until moistened. Using a pastry brush dipped in water, brush down inside of pan. Cook over medium-high heat, gently swirling pan just until sugar dissolves; cook, without stirring or swirling pan, until mixture is light amber colored.
3. Immediately remove from heat, and quickly stir in hazelnuts; pour onto prepared pan. Using a heatproof spatula, spread hazelnuts in a single layer; sprinkle with salt. Let cool completely.
4. Gently tap hazelnuts on baking sheet to break into smaller pieces, and chop with a chef's knife. Best used same day as made. Keep uncovered until ready to use.

Langues de Chat

Makes about 30 cookies

Langue de chat, French for "cat's tongue," is a classic French cookie that is crisp and buttery with a wonderful textural sensation thanks to the number of egg whites in the recipe. After baking, plunge these elegant cookies in a smooth ganache and decorate with dried fruit and candied citrus peel to add jeweled color and chewy texture.

½ cup (113 grams) unsalted butter, softened
½ cup (100 grams) granulated sugar
2 teaspoons (12 grams) vanilla bean paste
3 large egg whites (90 grams), room temperature
1 cup (125 grams) all-purpose flour
½ teaspoon (1.5 grams) kosher salt
Chocolate Ganache (recipe follows)
Garnish: chopped dried cranberries, chopped candied orange peel

1. Preheat oven to 400°F (200°C). Line baking sheets with parchment paper.
2. In the bowl of a stand mixer fitted with the paddle attachment, beat butter, sugar, and vanilla bean paste at medium speed until creamy, 3 to 4 minutes, stopping to scrape sides of bowl. Reduce mixer speed to medium-low. Add egg whites, one at a time, beating well after each addition.
3. In a medium bowl, sift together flour and salt three times. With mixer on low speed, gradually add flour mixture to butter mixture, beating just until combined. Spoon batter into a large pastry bag fitted with a medium round piping tip. Pipe batter onto prepared pans in straight lines about 3 inches long and ½ inch wide.
4. Bake until edges are golden brown, 8 to 12 minutes. Let cool completely on pans on wire racks.
5. Dip one end of cooled cookies in Chocolate Ganache, letting excess drip off; place on a sheet of parchment paper. Garnish with cranberries and orange peel, if desired. Let stand until chocolate is set, about 1 hour. Store in an airtight container for up to 5 days.

Chocolate Ganache

Makes about 1 cup

1 cup (170 grams) chopped bittersweet chocolate
¾ cup (180 grams) heavy whipping cream

1. In a medium heatproof bowl, place chocolate.
2. In a small saucepan, heat cream over medium-high heat just until bubbles form around sides of pan. (Do not boil.) Remove from heat; pour hot cream onto chocolate. Cover and let stand for 5 minutes; stir until chocolate is melted and mixture is smooth. Use immediately.

Gâteau Opéra

Makes 6 servings

The origins of this coffee- and chocolate-layered delight are uncertain. It's possible Louis Clichy created the first opera cake, a signature gâteau in his Paris shop. At the same time, Dalloyau, a pastry shop, sold a similar cake to honor the Paris Opera. To this day, the opera cake is a beloved classic with tender layers of almond sponge cake that are soaked in a rich coffee syrup. A bold Espresso French Buttercream and decadent chocolate ganache accompany the layers of cake, creating an unbeatable coffee-and-chocolate pairing. Covered in a stunning Chocolate Glaze, this dessert can't help but be the star of the show!

¾ cup (72 grams) blanched almond flour
½ cup (60 grams) confectioners' sugar
2 large eggs (100 grams)
3 large egg whites (90 grams)
¼ teaspoon cream of tartar
¼ cup (50 grams) granulated sugar
2½ tablespoons (20 grams) unbleached cake flour
1 tablespoon (14 grams) unsalted butter, melted and cooled slightly
1 teaspoon (4 grams) vanilla extract
2 ounces (57 grams) bittersweet chocolate, chopped
Coffee Syrup (recipe on page 176)
Espresso French Buttercream (recipe on page 176)
Ganache (recipe on page 176)
Chocolate Glaze (recipe on page 176)

1. Preheat oven to 400°F (200°C). Line a 17¼x12¼-inch rimmed baking sheet with parchment paper, letting excess extend over sides of pan.

2. In a medium heatproof bowl, sift together almond flour and confectioners' sugar. Add eggs, one at a time, whisking until well combined after each addition. Place bowl over a saucepan of simmering water; cook, whisking frequently, until an instant-read thermometer registers 95°F (35°C) to 105°F (41°C). Remove from heat, and whisk until light and ribbon-consistency. (Alternatively, beat with a hand mixer at medium-high speed until light and ribbon-consistency.)

3. In the bowl of a stand mixer fitted with the whisk attachment, beat egg whites and cream of tartar at medium speed until foamy. With mixer on medium speed, add granulated sugar in a slow, steady stream; increase mixer speed to medium-high, and beat until medium-stiff peaks form.

4. Add almond flour mixture to egg white mixture, and very gently fold until almost combined. (Mixture should look streaky.) Sift cake flour over egg mixture, and gently fold until just combined. Transfer about 1 cup (75 grams) batter to a small bowl, and fold in melted butter and vanilla. Add butter mixture to remaining batter, and fold until just combined. Pour large dollops across prepared pan, and gently spread into an even layer using as few strokes as possible.

5. Bake until golden and firm to the touch, 8 to 9 minutes. Let cool in pan for 10 minutes. Using excess parchment as handles, remove from pan, and let cool completely on parchment on a wire rack.

6. Move cake to a cutting board, and trim edges to create a 15x10½-inch rectangle. Discard edges. Cut into 3 (10½x5-inch) rectangles. Peel off parchment paper, and discard parchment. (Do not start soaking cake layers or assembling cake until syrup, buttercream, and ganache recipes are prepared and ready to be used.)

7. In a small microwave-safe bowl, heat chocolate on high for 30 seconds; stir chocolate. Heat on high in 15-second intervals, stirring between each, just until chocolate is melted.

8. Place 1 cake layer on a medium cutting board. Spread melted chocolate into an even layer on top of cake layer, being careful not to push it off layer onto cutting board. Refrigerate until firm, 5 to 10 minutes.

9. Turn cake layer so chocolate is on bottom. Place Coffee Syrup in a squeeze bottle, and soak cake layer with syrup. (If you do not have a squeeze bottle, use a pastry brush to soak cake layer.) Place half of Espresso French Buttercream (about 1 cup or 200 grams) into a pastry bag fitted with an extra-large ribbon piping tip (Ateco #898). (This is to make it easier to get an even layer of buttercream. If you do not have a ribbon tip, you can dollop and spread buttercream into an even layer.)

10. With flat side of piping tip facing up, pipe an even layer of buttercream on top of soaked cake layer; using a small offset spatula, smooth any lines. Place remaining Espresso French Buttercream in pastry bag, and set aside. Place second cake layer on top of buttercream layer, making sure it is even with bottom, and soak with Coffee Syrup. Dollop Ganache on top, and spread into an even layer. Top with remaining cake layer, and soak

continued . . .

. . . continued

with Coffee Syrup. Pipe remaining buttercream on top, and smooth flat. Place a piece of parchment paper on top of buttercream. Refrigerate until firm, about 1 hour, or freeze until firm, about 30 minutes.

11. Discard parchment. Place 2 tablespoons (30 grams) Chocolate Glaze into a parchment piping bag (see page 183). Quickly pour remaining Chocolate Glaze onto cold buttercream, tapping and lifting cutting board to help glaze settle and smooth out. (It's OK if some drips down the sides.) Let stand until set, 5 to 7 minutes. Cut a very small opening in tip of parchment piping bag, and pipe "Opera" (and designs, if desired) onto cake. Let stand until set, 5 to 7 minutes.

12. Using a hot dry knife, trim edges, cleaning knife between cuts. Cut into 6 slices. Serve immediately. (If not serving right away, cover and refrigerate for up to 5 days until ready to serve and then trim and slice. Let stand at room temperature to soften buttercream.)

Coffee Syrup

Makes about ¾ cup

- **½ cup (100 grams) granulated sugar**
- **½ cup (120 grams) water**
- **1 teaspoon (1 gram) instant espresso**
- **2 tablespoons (30 grams) cognac**

1. In a small saucepan, heat sugar and ½ cup (120 grams) water over medium heat, stirring constantly, until sugar dissolves. Stir in espresso. Remove from heat, and stir in cognac. Let cool completely before using.

Espresso French Buttercream

Makes about 2 cups

- **3 large egg yolks (56 grams), room temperature**
- **¾ cup (150 grams) granulated sugar**
- **3 tablespoons (45 grams) plus 1¾ teaspoons (9 grams) water, divided, plus more for brushing**
- **¾ cup plus 2 tablespoons (196 grams) unsalted butter, softened**
- **2½ teaspoons (2.5 grams) instant espresso**
- **¼ teaspoon kosher salt**

1. In a medium heatproof bowl, beat egg yolks with a hand mixer fitted with the beater attachments at medium-high speed until pale yellow and slightly thickened, 3 to 4 minutes.

2. In a small saucepan, stir together sugar and 3 tablespoons (45 grams) water; heat over medium heat until sugar dissolves. Using a pastry brush dipped in water, brush sides of pan to prevent sugar from crystallizing. Increase heat to high, and bring to a boil. (Do not stir.) Cook until an instant-read thermometer registers 240°F (116°C).

3. With mixer on low speed, slowly pour hot sugar syrup into egg yolk mixture in a slow, steady stream, being careful not to hit sides of bowl or mixer attachments; scrape sides of bowl. Increase mixer speed to high, and beat until bottom of bowl feels cool to the touch and mixture is very thick and very pale yellow, 4 to 5 minutes. Add butter, 1 tablespoon (14 grams) at a time, beating at medium speed until combined after each addition. (Mixture will look broken at times, but keep beating and it will come back together.)

4. In a small bowl, stir together espresso and remaining 1¾ teaspoons (9 grams) water. Add espresso mixture and salt to buttercream, and beat at low speed until combined, stopping to scrape sides of bowl. Use immediately.

Ganache

Makes about ⅔ cup

- **4 ounces (113 grams) bittersweet chocolate, finely chopped**
- **½ cup (120 grams) warm heavy whipping cream**

1. In the top of a double boiler, place chocolate. Heat, without stirring, over simmering water until almost melted. Gently stir until smooth. Remove from heat. Add warm cream, and starting in center of bowl, slowly stir with a rubber spatula until well combined. (Ganache will thicken as it cools.) Let stand until a spreadable consistency, about 15 minutes. (You can place in the refrigerator to help thicken faster; however, keep an eye on it so it doesn't get too thick and hard to work with.)

Chocolate Glaze

Makes about ⅔ cup

- **5 ounces (142 grams) bittersweet chocolate, finely chopped**
- **4 teaspoons (20 grams) neutral oil**

1. In the top of a double boiler, place chocolate. Heat, without stirring, over simmering water until almost melted. Gently stir until smooth. Remove from heat. Stir in oil. Let cool for 5 minutes before using.

Embracing the Joconde

The foundation of this cake is the almond joconde sponge, a classic French pastry element. It's nutty and rich but still as light as a sponge cake should be, creating the perfect base for our opera cake.

In a medium heatproof bowl, sift together almond flour and confectioners' sugar. Add eggs, one at a time, whisking until well combined after each addition. Place over a saucepan of simmering water; cook, whisking frequently, until an instant-read thermometer registers 95°F (35°C) to 105°F (41°C). Remove from heat, and whisk until light and ribbon-consistency. (Alternatively, beat with a hand mixer at medium-high speed until light and ribbon-consistency.)

TIP: The mixture should fall off the whisk in ribbons. For this step of the recipe, confectioners' sugar will dissolve more quickly and easily than granulated sugar. You can use a spoon or whisk to help push the almond flour and sugar through the sieve.

continued . . .

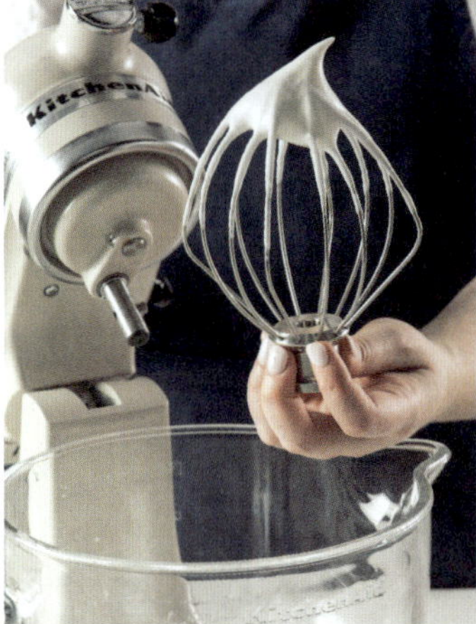

In the bowl of a stand mixer fitted with the whisk attachment, beat egg whites and cream of tartar at medium speed until foamy. With mixer on medium speed, add granulated sugar in a slow, steady stream; increase mixer speed to medium-high, and beat until medium-stiff peaks form.

TIP: Granulated sugar aids in the stabilization of the egg whites, but make sure you slowly add the sugar in a steady stream, which will ensure you don't deflate all the lovely air you whipped into the egg whites; it also helps make sure the sugar dissolves so you don't have textured meringue at the end.

Add almond flour mixture to egg white mixture, and very gently fold until almost combined. (Mixture should look streaky.) Sift cake flour over egg mixture, and gently fold until just combined. Transfer about 1 cup (75 grams) batter to a small bowl, and fold in melted butter and vanilla. Add butter mixture to remaining batter, and fold until just combined.

TIP: Lightly folding the eggs in at this step is key to a beautiful, airy sponge. Don't be tempted to get every bit of white and yolk folded together! Most importantly, make sure you don't overwork the batter. If you knock the air out of the eggs, the sponge won't rise properly.

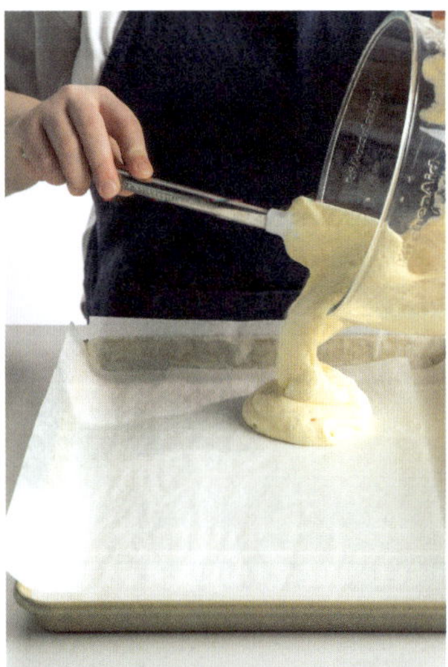

Pour large dollops across prepared pan, and gently spread into an even layer using as few strokes as possible.

TIP: Pouring the batter in dollops will help you in spreading the batter, but you also want to make sure you aren't deflating the batter as you spread it into the prepared pan.

Bake until golden and firm to the touch, 8 to 9 minutes. Let cool in pan for 10 minutes. Run a knife over any edges that may have clung to pan. Using excess parchment as handles, remove from pan, and let cool completely on parchment on a wire rack.

TIP: Using the excess parchment as a "sling" will help you transfer this delicate sponge with grace and ease!

Move cake to a cutting board, and trim edges to create a 15x10½-inch rectangle. Discard edges. Cut into 3 (10½x5-inch) rectangles. Peel off parchment paper, and discard parchment. Do not start assembling cake until syrup, buttercream and ganache recipes are prepared and ready to be used.

A Lovely Elixir

Espresso and cognac complement the flavor of chocolate as this syrup is brushed on the sponge cake layers

In a small saucepan, heat sugar and ½ cup (120 grams) water over medium heat, stirring constantly, until sugar dissolves. Stir in espresso. Remove from heat, and stir in cognac. Let cool completely before using.

TIP: Using a squeeze bottle for the Coffee Syrup will help you saturate the cake evenly with coffee and cognac, which are flavors that perfectly complement the chocolate and almond in this splendid cake.

Billowy Buttercream

The Espresso French Buttercream is beautifully balanced between the sweetness of the granulated sugar, the inherent depth and bitterness of espresso, and the richness of the unsalted butter

In a medium heatproof bowl, beat egg yolks with a hand mixer fitted with the beater attachments at medium-high speed until pale yellow and slightly thickened, 3 to 4 minutes.

TIP: Be patient during this step. You want to make sure the egg yolks have time to properly aerate.

In a small saucepan, stir together sugar and 3 tablespoons (45 grams) water; heat over medium heat until sugar dissolves. Using a pastry brush dipped in water, brush sides of pan to prevent sugar from crystallizing. Increase heat to high, and bring to a boil. (Do not stir.) Cook until an instant-read thermometer registers 240°F (116°C).

TIP: If the sugar granules that collect on the sides of the saucepan aren't brushed down, the sugar can harden and crystallize.

continued . . .

Billowy Buttercream *. . . continued*

With mixer on low speed, slowly pour hot sugar syrup into egg yolk mixture in a slow, steady stream, being careful not to hit sides of bowl or beater attachments; scrape sides of bowl. Increase mixer speed to high, and beat until bottom of bowl feels cool to the touch and mixture is very thick and very pale yellow, 4 to 5 minutes. Add butter, 1 tablespoon (14 grams) at a time, beating at medium speed until combined after each addition. (Mixture will look broken at times, but keep beating and it will come back together.)

TIP: As you are adding the butter to the egg yolk and sugar mixture, the butter should give just a slight resistance to the pressure of your fingers. If your butter is too cold, it can cause your buttercream to break. If you feel like your buttercream is too soft, which can happen if the butter is too warm or your egg mixture is not cool enough, refrigerate it for 15 to 30 minutes, or place the bowl over ice, stirring occasionally, and the buttercream will thicken nicely.

In a small bowl, stir together espresso and remaining 1¾ teaspoons (9 grams) water. Add espresso mixture and salt to buttercream, and beat at low speed until combined, stopping to scrape sides of bowl. Use immediately.

Gorgeous Ganache

Simple yet decadent, the ganache is the center layer, and its sweetness pairs beautifully with the bitter coffee notes

In the top of a double boiler, place chocolate. Heat, without stirring, over simmering water until almost melted. Gently stir until smooth. Remove from heat. Add warm cream, and starting in center of bowl, slowly stir with a rubber spatula until well combined. (Ganache will thicken as it cools.) Let stand until a spreadable consistency, about 15 minutes.

TIP: You can place in the refrigerator to help thicken faster; however, keep an eye on it so it doesn't get too thick and hard to work with.

Finishing Glaze

Straightforward and super smooth, this simple glaze made of bittersweet chocolate and neutral oil gives the cake a polished, elegant finish

In the top of a double boiler, place chocolate. Heat, without stirring, over simmering water until almost melted. Gently stir until smooth. Remove from heat. Stir in oil. Let cool for 5 minutes before using.
TIP: Adding oil to the melted chocolate re-emulsifies the chocolate and helps thin it out, creating a smooth, glossy finish that's easy to work with.

The Assemblage

Now that all the elements of the cake are ready, it's time for the finale

In a small microwave-safe bowl, heat chocolate on high for 30 seconds; stir chocolate. Heat on high in 15-second intervals, stirring between each, just until chocolate is melted.
TIP: Tempering the chocolate in the microwave will allow it to reharden and stay that way at room temperature. It acts as both a base for the cake and support for the cake-soaked layer.

Place 1 cake layer on a cutting board. Spread melted chocolate into an even layer onto cake layer, being careful not to push it off layer onto cutting board. Refrigerate until firm, 5 to 10 minutes.
TIP: Using an offset spatula will help spread the melted chocolate across the top layer of the cake effortlessly.

Turn cake layer so chocolate is on bottom. Place Coffee Syrup in a squeeze bottle, and soak cake layer with syrup. (If you do not have a squeeze bottle, use a pastry brush to soak cake layer.)
TIP: With the tempered base, you can move the assembled cake around easily with a large offset spatula.

continued . . .

The Assemblage *. . . continued*

Place half of Espresso French Buttercream (about 1 cup or 200 grams) into a pastry bag fitted with an extra-large ribbon piping tip (Ateco #898). With flat side of piping tip facing up, pipe an even layer of buttercream on top of soaked cake layer; using a small offset spatula, smooth any lines. Place remaining Espresso French Buttercream in pastry bag, and set aside. Place second cake layer on top of buttercream layer, making sure it is even with bottom, and soak with Coffee Syrup. Dollop Ganache on top, and spread into an even layer. Top with remaining cake layer, and soak with Coffee Syrup. Pipe remaining buttercream on top, and smooth flat. Place a piece of parchment paper on top of buttercream. Refrigerate until firm, about 1 hour, or freeze until firm, about 30 minutes.

TIP: This is to make it easier to get an even layer of buttercream. If you don't have a ribbon tip, you can dollop and spread buttercream into an even layer.

Discard parchment. Place 2 tablespoons (30 grams) Chocolate Glaze into a parchment piping bag. Quickly pour remaining Chocolate Glaze onto cold buttercream, tapping and lifting cutting board to help glaze settle and smooth out. (It's OK if some drips down the sides.) Let stand until set, 5 to 7 minutes. Cut a very small opening in tip of parchment piping bag, and pipe "Opera" (and designs, if desired) onto cake. Let stand until set, 5 to 7 minutes.

TIP: Be confident yet quick when spreading the glaze, as it will set speedily once it hits the cold buttercream. You should not have to spread the glaze if you move the board to distribute the glaze. This way, you won't have streaks, just a perfectly smooth surface. It's important for the glaze to be warm but not too hot so that the buttercream doesn't melt. Once the cake has had time to stand, it's a breeze to move to a serving platter, if you wish.

To make parchment piping bag: Fold a large piece of parchment paper in half diagonally, pressing firmly along the crease. Rotate the parchment to align the crease with the edge of your work surface. Cut the parchment along the seam with a knife, creating two triangles. Grab the far corner between your thumb and index finger and then roll the parchment around itself. Drag the paper until it forms a tight cone. While holding the cone in place with your right hand, lift up the loose parchment so you can slide your thumb under the cone to pinch it in place. With the cone secured between your right thumb and index finger, use your left hand to wrap the extra parchment around the cone until you have nothing left but a small flap that can be tucked into the body of the cone.

Using a hot dry knife, trim edges, cleaning knife between cuts. Cut into 6 slices. Serve immediately. (If not serving right away, cover and refrigerate until ready to serve and then trim and slice. Let stand at room temperature to soften buttercream.)

TIP: Simply run a knife under hot water and dry it off in between cuts to get perfect, smooth slices of cake.

Petit Fours

Makes 48 cakes

During the 19th century in France, bakers discovered they could utilize the residual warmth of their stone ovens after extinguishing the initial intense heat. This blazing hot setting used to bake crusty loaves of bread was called *grand four* or "big oven." The latent heat was enough to cook tiny, individual pastries as the oven cooled. This cooldown setting gave rise to the name *petit four* or "small oven," *et* voilà, the creation of petit fours! The small pastries eventually assumed the name of the oven setting they were baked in, and they've since been elevated into various small, exquisite pastries, now treasured worldwide.

---

1 cup (227 grams) unsalted butter, softened
1¾ cups (350 grams) granulated sugar
4 large eggs (200 grams), room temperature
¾ teaspoon (3 grams) almond extract
½ teaspoon (2 grams) vanilla extract
3 cups (375 grams) all-purpose flour
½ teaspoon (2.5 grams) baking powder
½ teaspoon (1.5 grams) kosher salt
¾ cup (180 grams) whole milk, room temperature
3 tablespoons (45 grams) sour cream, room temperature
Almond Buttercream (recipe follows)
White Chocolate Poured Fondant (recipe follows)
Garnish: edible gold leaf, melted white chocolate

1. Preheat oven to 325°F (170°C). Spray a 17½x12½-inch rimmed baking sheet with baking spray with flour. Line pan with parchment paper.
2. In the bowl of a stand mixer fitted with the paddle attachment, beat butter and sugar at medium speed until fluffy, 3 to 4 minutes, stopping to scrape sides of bowl. Add eggs, one at a time, beating well after each addition. Beat in extracts.
3. In a medium bowl, whisk together flour, baking powder, and salt. In a small bowl, whisk together milk and sour cream. With mixer on low speed, gradually add flour mixture to butter mixture alternately with milk mixture, beginning and ending with flour mixture, beating just until combined after each addition. Spread batter into prepared pan.
4. Bake until a wooden pick inserted in center comes out clean, 27 to 30 minutes. Let cool in pan for 10 minutes. Invert cake onto a wire rack, and discard parchment. Let cool completely.
5. Using a long serrated knife, trim cooled cake on all sides to create a 15x10-inch rectangle. Cut cake in half to create 2 (10x7½-inch) layers.
6. Spread half of Almond Buttercream (about ¾ cup or about 170 grams) on top of 1 cake layer. Top with remaining cake layer, lightly pressing to adhere. Spread remaining buttercream on second layer, smoothing as much as possible. Freeze for 1 hour. (Alternatively, tightly wrap assembled cake in plastic wrap, and freeze for up to 2 months. Unwrap cake, and let it thaw in the refrigerator overnight before proceeding.)
7. Using a long sharp knife, cut cake into 48 (1¼-inch) squares, and return to freezer.
8. Line a rimmed baking sheet with plastic wrap; place a wire rack on top. Place no more than 12 petit fours at least 1 inch apart on prepared rack. Carefully pour White Chocolate Poured Fondant onto petit fours, making sure all sides are completely covered, reheating and re-pouring fondant as necessary. (See Note.) Let stand until set, 10 to 15 minutes. Remove wire rack, spoon used fondant into liquid-measuring cup, and reheat as needed in the top of a double boiler or microwave to maintain a temperature range of 105°F (41°C) to 110°F (43°C).
9. Using a small offset spatula, move glazed petit fours to a serving platter. Repeat procedure with remaining petit fours and remaining White Chocolate Poured Fondant, only removing cakes from freezer when ready to pour. Garnish with gold leaf or melted white chocolate, if desired. Store in an airtight container for up to 2 days, or refrigerate in an airtight container for up to 1 week.

Note: *The glaze will seem far too thick to pour. If it is too warm, the glaze will simply slide off the cake and leave you with lumpy or translucent sides. It is OK if you pour more than is needed to achieve full coverage; the excess will drip off.*

Almond Buttercream

Makes about 1½ cups

½ cup (113 grams) unsalted butter, softened
1¾ cups (210 grams) confectioners' sugar
2 tablespoons (30 grams) heavy whipping cream
½ teaspoon (2 grams) almond extract
¼ teaspoon kosher salt

1. In the bowl of a stand mixer fitted with the paddle attachment, beat butter at medium speed until creamy, 2 to 3 minutes. Gradually add confectioners' sugar, beating until combined. Add cream, almond extract, and salt, beating until smooth, fluffy, and lightened in color and stopping to scrape bottom and sides of bowl and paddle.

White Chocolate Poured Fondant

Makes about 6 cups

10 cups (1,200 grams) confectioners' sugar
⅔ cup (226 grams) light corn syrup
⅔ cup (160 grams) water
2 teaspoons (8 grams) vanilla extract
2⅓ cups (397 grams) white chocolate chips

1. In the top of a double boiler, combine confectioners' sugar, corn syrup, ⅔ cup (160 grams) water, and vanilla. Cook over simmering water, whisking constantly, until smooth. Add white chocolate chips; cook, stirring frequently, until chocolate is melted and mixture is smooth. Reduce heat to low.
2. Spoon 2 cups (661 grams) fondant into a liquid-measuring cup. Let cool until an instant-read thermometer registers 105°F (41°C) to 110°F (43°C); use immediately.

Strawberry Petit Fours

Makes 48 cakes

Petit Fours batter (recipe on page 184)
½ cup (160 grams) strawberry preserves
¾ cup (170 grams) Almond Buttercream (recipe on page 184)
Poured Strawberry Fondant (recipe follows)

1. Proceed with Petit Fours recipe through step 5.
2. Spread preserves onto 1 cake layer. Top with remaining cake layer, lightly pressing to adhere. Spread Almond Buttercream on top in a smooth layer. Freeze for 1 hour. (Alternatively, tightly wrap assembled cake in plastic wrap, and freeze for up to 2 months. Unwrap cake, and let it thaw in the refrigerator overnight before proceeding.)
3. Continue Petit Fours recipe at step 7, using Poured Strawberry Fondant.

Poured Strawberry Fondant

Makes about 6 cups

10 cups (1,200 grams) confectioners' sugar
⅔ cup (226 grams) light corn syrup
½ cup (120 grams) water
¼ cup (80 grams) strawberry preserves, strained
2 teaspoons (8 grams) vanilla extract
2⅓ cups (397 grams) white chocolate chips
Pink liquid food coloring

1. In the top of a double boiler, combine confectioners' sugar, corn syrup, ½ cup (120 grams) water, preserves, and vanilla. Cook over simmering water, whisking constantly, until smooth. Add white chocolate chips; cook, stirring frequently, until chocolate is melted and mixture is smooth. Tint with food coloring as desired. Reduce heat to low.
2. Spoon 2 cups (661 grams) fondant into a liquid-measuring cup. Let cool until an instant-read thermometer registers 105°F (41°C) to 110°F (43°C); use immediately.

The Assemblage

Once the cake and the buttercream are made, it's time to assemble the petit fours

Using a long serrated knife, trim cooled cake on all sides to create a 15x10-inch rectangle. Cut in half to create 2 (10x7½-inch) rectangles.

Spread half of Almond Buttercream (¾ cup or 170 grams) on top of 1 cake layer. Top with remaining cake layer, lightly pressing to adhere. Spread remaining buttercream on second layer, smoothing as much as possible. Freeze for 1 hour.

Using a long sharp knife, cut cake into 48 (1¼-inch) squares, and return to freezer.
TIP: The freezer is your best friend when making petit fours, as these are easiest to slice and glaze after being chilled. Don't be tempted to skip this step or cut the freezing time in any way. If you do, the layers may slide around when slicing and the buttercream coating will melt when you glaze it with the warm poured fondant. If they sit in the freezer for too long and you notice some condensation has formed on the surface, don't fret. Simply blot the surface dry with a paper towel before glazing.

Master Poured Fondant

Poured fondant may sound intimidating, but it's a majestic, forgiving glaze. It gives petit fours a slightly lustrous appearance, yet they're dry to the touch and can be easily handled once set. The glaze beautifully gives way when bitten into, revealing the layers of cake and gorgeous filling.

Keep the glaze warm in a double boiler over low heat. The steam from the water underneath the bowl will heat the glaze just enough to keep it at that perfectly smooth and pourable consistency. Poured fondant hardens as it cools, but you don't want the glaze to set in the bowl before having time to coat each cake. To take the guesswork out of it, keep your eye on the temperature of the glaze using your trusty thermometer.

Pour a generous amount of glaze onto each petit four. The viscosity of the glaze pulls itself down the sides of the petit fours, creating an even coating. Don't worry about the excess glaze pooling at the bottom of the rimmed baking sheet under the wire rack; gently lift the plastic wrap and scrape the glaze back into the bowl, reheat, and reuse it!

If you notice your layer of glaze is uneven, don't be tempted to add more glaze. Pouring a second layer of glaze will only make it look more lopsided.

After glazing the petit fours, let them stand for 10 to 15 minutes to fully set before transferring them from the wire rack to a serving platter. Moving the petit fours too early will result in the glaze sliding around.

If you notice any bubbles forming in the glaze, simply use a wooden pick to pop it before the glaze has a chance to set fully.

Almond Gâteau Breton

Makes 1 (9-inch) cake

This traditional butter cake from Brittany, in northwest France, is one of the simplest of French cakes—it doesn't require layers, frosting, or any special equipment. I serve mine with a dab of Lemon Compote, but just about any fruit will work as a side to this elegant creation.

1¼ cups (250 grams) granulated sugar
½ cup (71 grams) whole blanched almonds, toasted
6 large egg yolks (112 grams)
1 cup (227 grams) unsalted butter, melted
2 cups (250 grams) all-purpose flour
1 large egg (50 grams)
2 teaspoons (10 grams) water
Lemon Compote (recipe follows)
Garnish: confectioners' sugar

1. Preheat oven to 325°F (170°C). Spray a 9-inch round cake pan with baking spray with flour.
2. In the work bowl of a food processor, process granulated sugar and almonds until finely ground, about 2 minutes.
3. In the bowl of a stand mixer fitted with the paddle attachment, beat egg yolks and sugar mixture at medium-high speed until thickened and light yellow, 3 to 4 minutes. Gradually add melted butter, beating until combined. Sift flour onto batter; stir just until combined (batter will be thick; do not overmix). Spread batter into prepared pan.
4. In a small bowl, whisk together egg and 2 teaspoons (10 grams) water; brush onto batter. Using a sharp knife, deeply mark a circular pattern in batter.
5. Bake until golden brown and a wooden pick inserted in center comes out clean, 30 to 35 minutes. Let cool in pan on a wire rack for 30 minutes. Serve with Lemon Compote. Garnish with confectioners' sugar, if desired. Store in an airtight container for up to 3 days.

Lemon Compote

Makes 1½ cups

½ cup (100 grams) granulated sugar
¾ cup (180 grams) almond liqueur
1 large lemon (99 grams), zested and sectioned
½ cup (85 grams) chopped candied ginger

1. In a medium saucepan, heat sugar over medium heat until golden in color. Remove from heat, and stir in liqueur. Return saucepan to medium heat; cook, stirring occasionally, until sugar is melted. Remove from heat; stir in lemon zest and sections and ginger. Let cool. Refrigerate in an airtight container for up to 1 week.

pro tip

To toast nuts, heat them in a dry skillet over medium heat, shaking frequently, until lightly browned and fragrant. Let cool completely before using.

French Apple Cake

Makes 1 (9-inch) cake

Layer upon layer of apple slices meld into a custardy cake batter that's spiked with spiced rum in this dessert inspired by classic Normandy Apple Cake.

---

7 cups (714 grams) ¼-inch sliced Honeycrisp apples
5 cups (520 grams) ¼-inch sliced Pink Lady apples
16 tablespoons (192 grams) granulated sugar, divided
1 tablespoon (15 grams) plus 1½ teaspoons (7.5 grams) dark rum, divided
1 teaspoon (5 grams) fresh lemon juice
3 large eggs (150 grams), room temperature
1½ teaspoons (6 grams) vanilla extract
1 cup (125 grams) all-purpose flour
1½ teaspoons (7.5 grams) baking powder
1 teaspoon (3 grams) kosher salt
¾ cup (170 grams) unsalted butter, melted and cooled
1 tablespoon (12 grams) sparkling sugar
Crème fraîche, to serve
Garnish: confectioners' sugar

1. Preheat oven to 400°F (200°C). Line 2 rimmed baking sheets with parchment paper. Butter a 9-inch round copper cake pan. (See Note.) Line bottom of pan with parchment paper; flour sides of pan.
2. In a large bowl, toss together apple slices, 2 tablespoons (24 grams) granulated sugar, 1 tablespoon (15 grams) rum, and lemon juice. Let stand for 15 minutes. Divide apple mixture between prepared baking sheets, spreading in a single layer.
3. Bake until apples have softened and released a lot of moisture, 20 to 30 minutes, stirring halfway through baking. (Apples will be slightly reduced in size but still retain their shape.) Let cool on pans for 20 minutes. Reduce oven temperature to 350°F (180°C).
4. In another large bowl, whisk eggs until pale and foamy, about 2 minutes. Add vanilla, remaining 14 tablespoons (168 grams) granulated sugar, and remaining 1½ teaspoons (7.5 grams) rum; whisk until well combined.
5. In a medium bowl, whisk together flour, baking powder, and salt. Gradually add flour mixture to egg mixture alternately with melted butter, beginning and ending with flour mixture, whisking just until combined after each addition.
6. Reserve 14 apple slices; fold remaining apple slices into batter. Using an offset spatula, spread batter in prepared cake pan, pressing down to distribute batter between apples and into edges of pan; smooth into an even layer. Arrange reserved 14 apple slices on top as desired; sprinkle with sparkling sugar.
7. Bake until golden brown and set, 1 to 1½ hours, covering with foil after 50 minutes of baking to prevent excess browning. Let cool completely in pan. Run a thin silicone or nylon offset spatula around edges of pan to loosen. Serve cake from pan using a nylon or silicone cake server, or transfer to desired serving plate. Serve with crème fraîche. Garnish with confectioners' sugar, if desired.

Note: *This recipe can also be made in a light-colored 9-inch springform pan. If using a springform pan, bake for 1 hour.*

index

index

credits

Editor-in-Chief Brian Hart Hoffman
EVP/Chief Content Officer
Brooke Michael Bell
Editorial Director Nancy Meeks
Art Director Liz Kight
Graphic Designer Kile Pointer
Associate Editor Amber Wilson
Assistant Editor Christina Fleisch
Senior Copy Editor, Food Meg Lundberg
Senior Digital Imaging Specialist
Delisa McDaniel

Test Kitchen Director Laura Crandall
Recipe Developers/Food Stylists
Ola Agbodza, Aaron Conrad,
Katie Moon Dickerson, Amanda Stabile
Contributing Recipe Developer/Food Stylist
Megan Lankford

Senior Stylist Sidney Bragiel
Stylists Maghan Armstrong, Courtni Bodiford,
Maggie Hill
Contributing Stylists Lucy Finney,
Mary Beth Jones

Photographers Jim Bathie, Kyle Carpenter,
John O'Hagan, Stephanie Welbourne Steele
Contributing Photographers
Stephen Devries (page 191), Mac Jamieson

Cover
Photography by Kyle Carpenter
Recipe Development by Megan Lankford
Food Styling by Katie Moon Dickerson
Styling by Sidney Bragiel

about the author

A former flight attendant and self-taught baker, Brian Hart Hoffman spent his early life traveling and discovering bakeries around the world, returning home with a mission to re-create the recipes. Brian launched an award-winning brand dedicated to the celebration of the global baking community: *Bake from Scratch*. Now, *Bake from Scratch* is one of the world's largest baking platforms, with magazines and best-selling cookbooks, a podcast (*The Crumb*), sell-out international and domestic baking retreats, and, of course, @thebakefeed on Instagram, a way for bakers around the world to connect.

Brian has authored numerous best-selling books, including *The Coupe*, *Holiday Coupetails*, *Fast-Fix Baking*, *The Bread Collection*, *The Pie & Tart Collection*, *The Cake Collection*, *The Cookie Collection*, *Holiday Cookies*, and *Bake from Scratch: Artisan Recipes for the Home Baker* volumes 1, 2, 3, 4, 5, 6, 7, and 8.